# ¡Carrera!

## How the world's greatest race got into my head and kicked my butt

## Mike McNessor

To Kathy, Kim, Ken, Billie Jo, Scott, Lisa, Steve, Mom, Dad and Mick, thanks for everything.

During the year-long process of planning, talking about and obsessing over
La Carrera Panamericana, I received many words of encouragement from some terrific people...

**"You guys need to stop talking about it and just do it."**

*My wife, Kathleen McNessor*

**"Stop sweating the little details and make sure you've got the major stuff covered."**

*Gerie Bledsoe, Former North American coordinator for La Carrera Panamericana and a winner of the Historic C division*

**"Mike, we're doing this. I don't care if I have to pay for all of it."**

*Kim Sterritt*

**"You have the beginning symptoms of a very long, long sickness, my friend. This race... it infects you."**

*LaCarrera mentor, sponsor and perennial Carrera racer Jose Rubio*

# Contents

# Preface
## The Idea that wouldn't quit

**F**or almost 10 years I did everything possible to hide from this book. I changed jobs, disguised myself by losing weight (then gained most of it back), cut my thinning hair short and went grayer than a two-term American President. But no matter how much I tried to avoid it, *The Idea* wouldn't quit pestering me. Neither, fortunately, would my wife Kathy, aka "The Chief." Her constant reminders that I'd been talking about writing a book for years but hadn't delivered enough text to fill a sympathy card, (*Sorry for your loss of ambition*) made me feel guilty enough to finally sit down in front of my computer and gape at car parts for sale on the internet when I should've been writing a book.

Now that this work of literature is finished, I'm not really sure what category it falls into: Nonfiction, Memoir, Grandiose Delusion, Manifesto, Word Salad? Whatever. At this point, with so much time in the rearview mirror, I just wanted to do it, so I could say I did it. Just like La Carrera Panamericana. There really is no point, it's just a way to drown out the sound of life's ticking clock for a few fun moments.

The story that follows jumps around a little. It starts with what very little I know about La Carrera Panamericana and why it became an obsession for a couple years of my life. Then, there's some deep background about your esteemed author, followed by thank yous to everyone who was conned into helping me participate in the Carrera. I also included information about how some of these folks became unfortunate enough to know me. (Hopefully this knowledge will help you avoid people like me in your own life.) The rest mostly focuses on our race preparation and experiences — all of which I'd advise *against* using as guide for your own vintage racing adventures.

Anyway, thanks, for picking up this book and attempting to wade through it. I hope you enjoy it.

# Chapter 1
## Beer and car magazines don't mix

Y ou've probably heard this story a zillion
times. A couple of guys get liquored up,
buy a crappy old Cold War era Chevrolet,
weld in a roll cage, convert the engine, for some
unknown reason, to run on propane and then flog
said Chevrolet relentlessly from one end of Mexico to
the other.

Well, almost.

The end.

Oh. You haven't?

I'll warn you, that some of the particulars of this
adventure are sketchy in my mind, at best. Like all the

words to Ritchie Valens' *La Bamba*. Except, of course, "*La Bamba*." Or that promise I make to myself every day about cutting back on the beer and potato chips about two hours after I make it.

Oh right, I was going to be healthier starting today. But today was *sooooo* hard. Great, it's settled then... I'll start tomorrow. Or maybe not.

Squinting back through the fog, I remember my buddy Kim and I getting fairly hammered one June night, and scoffing at a story in a car magazine describing how abusive Mexico's La Carrera Panamericana can be on men, women, vehicles, household budgets, personal relationships, etc.

"Bah! How tough can it really be? The guy who wrote that article is a *wuss*!" we agreed, our confidence fortified by liquified hops and barely.

The more beer we drank on that June night, the more convinced we became that the author was a sun-dress-wearing candy ass who couldn't hang with either of us if his half-witted, pretty-boy, car-magazine-writing life depended on it.

At least that's how I remember it. After sleeping it off, I picked up the phone and called Kim.

Twenty seconds into the conversation — sober,

for the moment — I was harassing my friend like a starving telemarketer trying to sell him on the idea of entering the big Mexican Road Race.

"Look, I think I can get us a trailer, a truck and maybe even a guy to drive it. I also think I can land us enough sponsorship money that we won't have to do this totally out of pocket."

"Mike, you're serious about this?" Kim asked, sounding justifiably leery of the lunatic on the other end of the phone. "Do you really think you can get us that stuff for nothing?"

"Of course!" was my answer.

*Hmmmm... good question,* was what I was thinking.

At the time, I was lucky enough to work at a really good daily newspaper, the Albany, N.Y. *Times Union,* where serious, dedicated journalists were writing stories that exposed injustice and corruption, or broke news of vital importance to the community.

Meanwhile, I was writing jokey reviews of new cars, SUVs and trucks often exposing how much of a moron I can be to the 10 or 15 readers who might've been paying attention. The word "scam" comes to mind when comparing this job to the occupations that I was legitimately qualified for: airport parking

valet and shuttle bus driver (my first paying job out
of college); building materials handling flunky and
truck driver (my job during high school and college);
cleaner of dead person's house (one of my first paying jobs, ever).

I'd grown up reading car magazines and always
wanted to write and photograph cars for a living. Writing was the one thing at which I was even
remotely competent and my English teachers in high
school as well as my college literature professors
always encouraged me to pursue it. And by "encouraged" I mean I didn't fail their classes the way I usually failed math, science and pretty much everything
else except metal shop.

Look, I know I'll never be a Mark Twain, James
Thurber or Kurt Vonnegut but, like those literary
greats, I've experienced the rush of reading my work
aloud and hearing an entire room erupt in laughter.
So what if those guys were on a stage reading in front
of an audience of hundreds of people and I was all
alone in my spare bedroom? Even self-inflicted laughter is laughter.

My position at the *Times Union* was so awesome
because, in addition to a paycheck, health insurance

and the omelet station at the company cafeteria, it gave me access to the coveted auto manufacturers' press fleet and its all-you-can-eat smorgasbord of free cars and trucks to drive and review.

Each week, a new car, truck, SUV or whatever would roll into the parking lot at the office, dripping with spray wax, glass cleaner and tire shine, its fuel gauge pinned on full and tuned up to do with as I pleased for seven glorious, unsupervised days. At the end of the week, another brand-new vehicle, detailed and brimming with fuel, would magically arrive and the cycle of addiction continued.

To occasionally break up the monotony of having free, unlimited use of new cars and trucks, auto manufacturers would send me on all-expense-paid trips to exotic locations, where I could stuff myself full of free gourmet food and booze, then be swaddled in 10,000-thread-count sheets before being tossed the keys to the latest model for a few dreamy days of luxury touring.

The nice public relations people who arrange these trips and deliver the new vehicles on behalf of car manufacturers are apparently instructed to treat every hack blogger or part-time weekly newspaper columnist like he's Rupert Murdoch, wielding the power to crush the fortunes of a global automobile company with one unfavorable remark about the way a vehicle's lumbar support pressed uncomfortably against his overfed blogger ass.

Believe me when I tell you that when you're on the receiving end of this coordinated, orchestrated and well-funded royal treatment it can become intoxicating. *Yes, yes,* you begin to delude yourself, *my stupid observations about a vehicle's cup holders and the complexity of its "infotainment system" truly do matter to people other than Mom and, when he's in the market for a new Lexus, my dentist.*

For a dork from upstate New York who, as a teenager, used to spend his spare time dawdling over newsstands pawing the latest issues of *Hot Car, Rod Craft* or *Autos and Drivers* as well as cruising car lots to ogle the new Camaros, Corvettes or Mustangs after the salespeople had all gone home, being treated to a fleet of new vehicles and flown to one new-car driving experience after the next was the like becoming an overnight member of Led Zeppelin.

Of course, there are definite hierarchies assigned to the various media outlets. For instance, the guys at

*Car Trend* and *Motor Driver* with their 1 million-plus
circulations are the A listers and get opportunities that
Y and Z listers like me could only daydream about
during quiet moments waiting at the company cafeteria's omelet station. As an example, when the Cadillac
CTS-V was released, GM built a racing version of the
car and campaigned it in the Speed World Challenge
series, to prove that the car was as track capable as
high-performance German sedans. To get some
publicity for the race team, journalists were given different degrees of access to the howling 3,000-pound
500-plus horsepower race cars. One editor working at
a well-known magazine drove an actual CTS-V race
car on a road course and wrote a feature story comparing it to competition versions of the Audi RS6,
Viper and Corvette, which the writer of that story
also drove.

Meanwhile Mike McNessor, the knucklehead from
the local newspaper, was given one lap around Lime
Rock in a passenger's seat that had been temporar-
ily installed in the racing CTS-V with Cadillac factory driver and insane Italian person, Max "The Ax"
Angelelli at the wheel doing his honest best to give
me something to write about.

Hey, I'm not complaining — it beat spending the afternoon cleaning expired canned goods out of a dead lady's kitchen pantry. But, the point is, I hardly wanted to spend my entire career writing about my experiences in the most awesome cars of the world as viewed from the passenger's seat.

By the same token, as freaking awesome as it was getting new cars to drive every week, I didn't want to live out my days staring at a blank computer screen, wringing my brain for an original phrase to describe the abundance of console storage compartments in the latest sport-utility, crossover, whatever-in-the-name-of-Christ vehicle some of these new cars are supposed to be. Seriously, once you've written about one all-wheel-drive, jellybean shaped, four-door, what's-its-thing perched on big tires so people don't feel like they're driving a minivan, you've written about them all. And that's about all that carmakers seem to be able to sell these days.

So, if Kim and I made it the 7,000 or so miles to this race and back, perhaps I could whip it into a pretty good road trip story. Maybe someone would even be willing to associate themselves with us as a sponsor in return for whatever publicity I could generate about our antics.

All things considered, the Carrera is a good value, but it's still fairly expensive. The entry fee when we participated in 2004 was $4,500, which is reasonable, considering it included meals and a week's worth of stays in very nice hotels. But a race car can quickly become a credit card company's best friend. Even the most basic setup will wind up costing you $15,000 to assemble, doing everything yourself (or with the help of caring friends and relatives), cutting corners and scrounging junkyard parts. Then you can throw at least another $3,000 on this money fire getting to the race, if you don't live in or near Mexico, for fuel, tolls, snacks, alimony payments, etc.

I immediately went to work on several of my contacts in the automotive world to see how much they would be willing to pay for the dubious distinction of putting their names on a race car we had yet to locate and purchase.

Answer: Nothing, nada, zip. Cue the crickets.

I was certain, at least, that one of the major automobile manufacturers would be more than happy to lend us a tow vehicle. After all, the writer of the magazine article that first introduced me to La Carrera

Panamericana had borrowed his truck from the press fleet.

No way. For a 5,000-plus-mile tow across the Mexican border and hopefully back? Uh, uh, they all told me.

Ah yes, that's right. I'd become so intoxicated on the free booze and spray wax fumes that I'd forgotten my place. The guy who'd gotten a truck from the press fleet for his story about La Carrera Panamerica was a car magazine A-lister.

Even my employers at the *Times Union* treated my requests for financial support, in exchange for a series of articles, as if they were scam emails from the lawyer of a wealthy Nigerian Prince. My boss, apparently not familiar with Gonzo Journalism, accused me of trying to whore out my position at the newspaper for personal gain.

Whoa, was that what I was doing? I'd read stories exactly like this in car magazines my entire life. I never saw any of those guys as whores. Undisciplined hacks maybe, but whores?

After some serious thought, I decided I really didn't care. La Carrera Panamericana is the single greatest automotive adventure of a lifetime: A chance to drive flat out on Mexico's roads, staring wide-eyed over the steely dashboard of a dangerous, Cold War-era, Detroit dinosaur. Cripes, I might not live long enough to flagrantly squander fossil fuels like this ever again.

Fortunately I'd managed to sell one person on this questionable idea. One cool November night, just before Kim—who was working as an engineer in the Merchant Marines—shipped out for a few months aboard a massive container ship, my longtime friend told me he didn't care about sponsors.

"We're doing this, Mike," he said. "Even I have to pay for all of it."

Of course, if you purchased this book you have signed on as a sponsor, albeit retroactively. I've never told this entire story anywhere else because I always wanted to do it long form, make it my first attempt at writing a book and hopefully sell a few copies to help pay for continued improvements to the 1961 Impala we bought, built and raced.

So, muchas gracias (that's how they say "thank you," I think, in Mexico), dear reader, for your support. Grab a beer and we'll toast: To La Carrera Panamericana! And seriously — tomorrow, I'm cutting back on the alcohol and potato chips.

# Chapter 2

## Mexico: Bring us your crazies yearning to speed

**N**ever heard of La Carrera Panamericana? Yeah, well, for me too it was just another of about 10 million things that happens in foreign countries of which I am blissfully ignorant. But unlike the Running of the Bulls or professional soccer, this business of driving old cars at high speeds on public roads was enough to make me update my passport. Was it really possible that some goofball from Upstate New York could take a pre-1965 Chevy down to Mexico and be considered a race car driver?

It's all true and then some…

With the approval of the Federales as well as the

Army and local police agencies throughout Mexico, people from all over the world, in cars 1965 and older, run like hell from one end of Mexico to the other.

When we participated, the race route snaked through the majestic mountains of the state of Chiapas in the south, at times soaring as high as 9,000 feet, through the urban congestion of Mexico City and across the expansive desert flats of the north.

The Carrera was run over seven days covering 200-400 miles per day. Every night the race finished in a new picturesque town, whose citizens threw a street celebration and flocks of local people turned out to eyeball the colorful classic cars. Carrera racers were asked for autographs and pumped for information about their cars and the race. Afterward, you headed back to your hotel and used the downtime to whip your battle-worn race car back into shape for the next day's pounding, or you just hung out, commiserating with your crew and the other racers.

Every morning, driver, co-driver and crew had to roll out of bed, quickly shake off whatever side effects were lingering from the previous day's thrashing, and report to the starting arch ready to run flat on the mat all day long, all over again.

In the United States, such a hedonistic display of amateur motorsports would have the safety police forming torch-wielding mobs and lawyers slithering out from under their rocks in search of litigants. But Mexico's drivers turn over their country's roads to the Carrera with little more than a shrug, waiting out brief traffic delays and giving racers the right of way with a smile and a wave.

Driving in Mexico seemed to afford a lot of opportunities for going way too fast, but the Carrera organizers saw to it that everyone got a full speed fix. Each of the seven days' rally-racing festivities are divided into speed and transit stages.

During the speed stages, long stretches of diabolically twisted roads are closed off to public traffic and racers are permitted to drive as fast as they dare. The year we competed, some dared to drive so fast that they ran off the road and slammed into unforgiving fixtures of the Mexican countryside—like trees or rocks the size of Aztec Pyramids.

Others drove more slowly and carefully, so as not to wad their fragile old 1961 Impala race car into an unidentifiable lump of amateurishly prepared scrap metal.

The transit stages are long stretches of public road that connected the speed stages. One might assume that, during these portions, the tendency would be to drive at or perhaps slightly above the posted speed limit (as the race rule book suggested). One would be wrong. Driving antics that would earn you handcuffs and a ride in the back of a patrol car in the U.S. were standard operating procedure. It's not just the racers either. Mexico's motorists tend to drive fast and pass freely, anywhere on most roads. A thick pack of oncoming traffic doesn't deter the average driver in Mexico from passing the car in front of him. But instead of a road rage incident braking out, everyone just moves over to make more room. Three cars wide on a two-lane road? Sure, why not?

During the Carrera, especially in the later stages, you had to run your car wide open to stay on schedule. Our race car could only manage about 110-120 mph on the mat, but we ran it there plenty. We would've done it more often, had the engine not been so prone to boiling over in the scorching heat.

While the modern version of the great Mexican Road Race is grueling on drivers and co-drivers, the original race was a meat grinder.

From its inaugural running in 1950, as a stunt to promote Mexico's newly opened, state-of-the-art Panamerican Highway, until its swan song in 1954, well-funded factory teams and privateers fielding brand-new or nearly new automobiles competed for enough cash to buy a half-dozen new American sedans of the day. The original race started in Juarez, Mexico, and wound its way south on the Pan American highway, 2,135 miles to the Guatemalan border. In 1950, Portland, Oregonian Hershel McGriff, who went on to distinguish himself in NASCAR racing, flattened the 132-car field with a 1950 Oldsmobile two-door. McGriff and his co-driver, Ray Elliot, averaged a blistering 78.421 mph and finished the race in 27 hours, 34 minutes and 25 seconds, according to an Associated Press report of the day. For his efforts, McGriff netted $17,381 in prize money. Tough? Of the 132 cars that started the race only 58 finished. Which is like half, or something. (If only I hadn't flunked Math.)

The first of the original Carrera's many fatalities occurred just 17 miles from the starting line on Cinco de Mayo 1950. From there the bodies piled up, drivers and spectators alike, until the plug was pulled after the 1954 race. One report of the day also blames American car companies, sick of taking a backseat for the overall win to Ferrari and Mercedes Benz, for the Carrera's demise.

In 1988, a group resurrected the infamous race and have run it annually as a vintage rally ever since. It's still no old-car parade — people have been seriously injured in the modern event. But it's extremely well-orchestrated and safety is the highest priority.

To win the race today would take more cash and experience, than I'll ever possess. The top cars are built like NASCAR stock cars and bodied to look like old Studebakers, Oldsmobiles or whatever. The racers wheeling them are multi-time Carrera competitors with serious crews and money to spend.

These days, the winners get no cash and prizes for their efforts, just a trophy presented by some pretty girls. However, this probably helps keep the frenzy of competition to a minimum.

The cool thing about the Carrera is that it's open to anyone who can prepare a car according to the rules, or purchase one already prepared and get it to the starting stripe. There were no driving schools, nor licensing classes required when we participated.

Today's Carrera racers are tough, but the original competitors were total badasses. Pictured here, during the 1954 event, Lincoln driver Walt Faulkner and his navigator Frank Hainley wrestle on a fresh set of bias plys as local residents look on. Check out the safety gear: Special-issue Lincoln team T-shirts tucked neatly into chinos and what appear to be polo helmets.
— PHOTO COURTESY OF FORD MOTOR CO.

If you've got the money, the car and the time, you can be a real racer in a big V-8-powered machine — complete with requests from spectators for autographs and everything. Check it out at www.panamrace.com or the race's official site, www.lacarrerapanamericana.com.mx. Then grab a copy of my current employer's flagship publication, *Hemmings Motor News*, (or www.hmn.com) and get searching for a suitable car.

Nobody really cares if you're just a goofball from upstate New York, barely able to scrape up lunch money most of the time. In Mexico, you are a racer.

# Chapter 3
## A go kart as a gateway drug

**B**y now you've probably surmised that I'm a textbook candidate for psychotherapy. Narcissistic. Bipolar. Irrational fears of having to actually work for a living. The works. In literary terms, an "unreliable narrator." In everyday terms, an "automotive journalist."

I've somehow avoided the therapist's couch so far, but from what I understand, therapy sometimes involves medication and blaming your parents for your own pathetic inadequacies.

But my parents... well, they're just good, hardworking people. They did their honest best with what they had to work with. You can't build an Indy 500 winner out of a 1976 Nova four-door and you can't make Chicken Francese out of chicken manure.

Medication? I can grab everything I need after work at The Beverage Den, including a bag of kettle cooked potato chips (tomorrow, I'm totally off those things) and the latest issue of *Chevy Muscle Fever Illustrated*. No copay required.

I don't think my parents should be allowed to get off scot-free though. It is basically because of them that you traded some of your lunch money to read the delusional ravings of a lunatic. There are no returns on this book either, by decree of the publisher (me) so the way I see it, my parents owe you a ham and cheese sandwich, and maybe a pickle, minimum.

It was Mr. and Mrs. McNessor who unintentionally put a lot of the still-to-this-day bad ideas in my head when they bought me my very first race car: A stripped down, open-wheel special with a mid-mounted engine and a tubular chassis.

When I first laid eyes on it, this new-to-me go kart was parked in the back of my old man's 1975 Chevrolet pickup. My parents bought it from one of our neighbors, who'd probably built it following plans

in *Mechanix Illustrated*, circa 1962, and poached the
5hp Tecumseh engine from a garage-sale rototiller.
It wasn't running when we took ownership of it, but
it was obviously a "diamond in the rough." And by
"diamond" of course I mean, "a pile of junk."

You see, we McNessors are a people whose family
history is steeped in a proud tradition of buying der-
elict project vehicles and mechanical eyesores. If we
had a family coat of arms, on it would be a rusty '69
Chevelle propped up on cement blocks with "MAKE
OFFER" scrawled across the windshield in white
shoe polish. Next to the car there would be a swap
meet table covered with used hand tools marked,
"Dirt Cheap! Everything Must Go!"

For instance, your first bicycle, or the first bicycle
you bought for your kid, might've come from a bike
shop, off the rack at a department store or maybe
used from somebody's garage sale. It could've been a
hand-me-down from an older sibling.

My first bicycle just sort of appeared in the garage
one day, the way a pimple just appears on a kid's face,
sporting a fresh, gleaming coat of Mack Truck-brand
red enamel (My Dad was an owner-operator trucker).
Accenting the still-tacky red paint: a new red banana

seat and handle grips as well as a curious patina of rust over most of the chrome surfaces. The tires too looked sort of dry rotted and shot. I guess I just assumed that this sort of oxidation and decay was normal on new bicycles and never questioned it until I met a couple of the older neighborhood kids while out for a ride.

"Hey, that's my old bike!" one of them said.

"Huh?" I replied, confused as usual.

"Yeah, we took it to the dump last weekend!"

Before my face could turn roughly the same shade of Mack Red as my refurbished bicycle, the kid's friend said something that surprised me and grotesquely warped my perspective for the rest of my life:

"Man, but it looks really cool now! Did you paint it and put that new seat on?"

"Uh no, my Dad did."

"Wow, awesome job!"

"Uh, yeah... thanks!"

That was all the validation I needed. From then on, I was certain that my bike was vastly superior to any sissy store-bought bike and I soon began customizing it further. The 1970s BMX craze was in full swing, as

I learned watching a BMX-themed episode of *CHiPs*, so I put on a set of black low-rise handlebars with a crossbar as well as a black solo seat in place of the red banana saddle my old man had installed. I scuffed off the red paint and sprayed on a fresh coat of rattle-can silver — my first paint job! That bike carried me to many a respectable lap on the makeshift BMX course we set up in my neighbor's old cow pasture. I'm not sure what happened to that bike, but hopefully it never found its way to the dump again.

My go-kart too was a fixer upper. The Tecumseh ran when we pulled it out of the back of my Dad's pickup but it was hobbled by a broken centrifugal clutch and a missing throttle cable. It was summer vacation, so while I was waiting to get the necessary parts and for my Dad to fix it, I would go out in the garage and stare at my kart, dreaming of how I would paint and letter it up like a real racing machine.

I'd seen Don "The Snake" Prudhomme run a match race at the area drag strip, Lebanon Valley Dragway, with his Army-sponsored Funny Car, so that's probably where I drew my inspiration: I'd paint it red, white and blue and call it the *American Challenger*, I thought. A good, wholesome, patriotic name to inspire the legions of fans I'd someday wow with my daring exploits of driving danger in my parents' backyard.

This was before I'd gone all out customizing my bicycle like the ones on the BMX episode of *CHiPs*, so building the *American Challenger* was still a little beyond my capabilities and unfortunately it never really got out of the concept stage. I knew that no real *American Challenger* would have seat cushions upholstered with floral-print fabric like my kart was cursed with though, so the first change I made was to rip that girlie stuff off, leaving just the bare plywood seat. Good enough, real racers don't need to be pampered with fancy prints.

Once, while I was gazing at the *American Challenger*, dreaming of the day I'd wheel it into Victory Lane, one of my sister's friends, a guy named Rick, came out with my sister for a look.

"Cool kart! You going to fire it up and drive it?" Rick asked.

"Nah, can't right now, it's broken." I said.

"Well, what's wrong with it?"

"The centrifugal clutch is frozen so it tries to move as soon as you pull the engine over and the throttle cable needs to be hooked up to the gas pedal."

"Hmmm…" Rick looked around and spied my old man's Snap-On tool chest. He walked over and grabbed a set of hex keys out of one of the drawers then came back and knelt alongside the clutch. I looked on in awe as he backed out the screws holding on the clutch cover and pulled it off revealing a broken spring inside.

"Here, I'll bet this busted spring was stuck between the clutch shoes causing it to stick. It should move with just two springs."

Rick tugged at the pull cord and the Tecumseh popped to life settling into a crackling idle. He grabbed the loose end of the throttle cable and pointed it at me.

"The cable is too short to reconnect to the gas pedal, but you could just pull on it a little when you want to go faster," Rick said, his voice now raised so he could be heard over the *American Challenger's* snarling, rototiller exhaust note. "Go on, take it for a ride!"

I swung myself onto the hard plywood seat, hardly able to believe that I was taking my first lap. Just a shakedown run of course, to get the bugs out of both driver and machine, but one for the history books.

Would someday Rick and my sister, tears streaming down their cheeks, tell Chris Economaki on the *Wide World of Sports*, that they had witnessed the birth pangs of one of auto racing's greatest legends, perhaps as I wheeled my stock car, the *American Challenger II*, into the Daytona 500 Winner's Circle? The thrill of victory, indeed.

I pulled gently on the throttle cable and the kart inched forward toward the open garage door and perhaps, destiny. Once in the driveway, I "blipped" the throttle (a term I'd read in magazines) and began picking up speed. It was difficult driving with only my left hand on the wheel and my right hand tugging the severed throttle cable. If I could just get my right hand on the wheel too, I thought, it'd be easier to drift the *American Challenger* around the unpaved cul de sac my old man had built in our yard to make it easier to turn his dump truck around. So, still holding the throttle cable in my right hand, I stretched my arm toward the steering wheel. This had the unintended effect of raising the engine rpm and increasing the *American Challenger's* speed. Panic! I was on a collision course with a giant pile of sand that my father had dumped in the yard, so, still gripping the cable,

I yanked the wheel hard to the left to avoid it. The action pulled the throttle wide open unleashing the Tecumseh's full 5hp fury. The front wheels were full lock, pointing away from the sand pile, but the rear-heavy kart plowed straight ahead.

Whuuuff.

The *American Challenger* augured into the sand pile, like the rototiller its engine had once powered. It seemed as if I'd blasted into the dirt at 80 mph, though it was probably more like .0008 mph. Nevertheless, the force of the impact threw my butt up out of the seat and planted me, face first, into the sand. Rick and my sister soon arrived on the scene of this grisly crash and did what anyone would do after witnessing an eight-year-old boy ramming a go kart into a giant pile of sand: They laughed, tears streaming down their cheeks, to the point of nearly soiling themselves. And there it was, my first vehicular humiliation in what would become a long life of vehicular and various other types of humiliation. The agony of defeat, indeed.

Unfortunately, my half-gainer into the dirt had little to no effect on my confidence or my optimism for a future of driving glory. American pop culture of the

1970s and '80s and even my parents, to some degree, led me to believe that every day of my adult life was going to be like an episode of *The Dukes of Hazzard*.

*Aha!* You're probably saying. *Finally, THIS is the part of the book where McNessor starts blaming his parents for his numerous pathetic shortcomings as a human being.*

But no, I would reply, if this weren't an imaginary conversation we're having, I'm not exactly blaming them.

*Bummer*, you're saying, *I thought this book was finally going to be worth reading.*

Nope, I'd reply in this imaginary conversation, I'm afraid this is about as good as it gets.

If there was anybody in the world I idolized it was my old man. Still do. He's one of those guys who can build a garage, then drag broken stuff inside — town-dump-rescued bicycles, old cars, bulldozers, front end loaders, dump trucks, etc. — and completely rebuild them. He has endless energy and pit bull tenacity combined with otherworldly mechanical skills.

But throughout my childhood, my father told a lot of stories about drag racing on the streets around our town in the 1960s. As near as I can tell, there were no laws governing the operation of motor vehicles in Upstate New York back then and drag races were just part of the normal flow of traffic. Maybe even a required skill needed to get a license, like parallel parking or hand signals.

**1960s Upstate NY DMV Road Test**

**Administrator:** *OK, using your hand signals, indicate a right turn, pull to the curb then parallel park. When you're finished, I want you to pull alongside that guy in the Dodge and tell him his car is a slow pile of junk that couldn't outrun a cement mixer.*

My old man didn't mean to put a lot of stupid ideas into my head, he was just trying to share funny, exciting stories about cars with his son. Plus, he'd always end his tales with the disclaimer: "Of course, you can't get away with that kind of stuff nowadays." As a trucker in the golden age of trucking, he was a daily user of the CB radio and knew that radios were the lifeblood of police traffic patrols. "And you can't outrun the radio," he'd say.

It wasn't just my old man, it was almost like everyone I knew considered *Smokey and the Bandit* to be one of the most influential documentaries of our age. Cars were made for driving fast on public streets and the police were just a pain in the ass. Getting chased by the police was just another male rite of passage, like having sex for the first time, or as it turned out for me, adult circumcision.

It was late on a Sunday night. I was 19, stupid and full of testosterone. A couple of kids in a rattle-trap Mustang pulled alongside my Chevy Monte Carlo winter-beater at a red light. For no apparent reason, that I can recall, the Mustang's passenger leaned out of his window and hocked a fairly substantial loogie on my car. My cousin and his friend — the son of a retired New York State Trooper — had the misfortune of being my passengers in my car. They were older than me and I wanted to seem cool to them, so I decided it would be a good idea to chase this guy down and find out why he couldn't keep his spit to himself. Sooner that you can think, *this is going to end badly*, we were westbound on Central Avenue, side by side at 75 mph in a 30 mph zone. Then, 30 seconds after I'd caught up to the Mustang, an Albany Police cruiser passed us in the eastbound lane.

Uh oh.

The cop pulled a fast U-turn in his Dodge Diplomat patrol car and turned on his red lights. The guy driving the Mustang and his friend, the spitter, made the wise decision to pull to the side of the road. Meanwhile, I saw this as my golden opportunity to join the proud fraternity of scholars and wise men who'd led police on high-speed pursuits, as seen in all of their splendor on almost any episode of *COPS*.

Secretly, almost 30 years later, I still wish this story could end with me — the cunning young country bumpkin — gloriously out driving and outwitting a pack of police cars, just like Burt Reynolds in that black Pontiac Trans Am in *Smokey and the Bandit.*

But my life has never really been about beating anyone at anything — particularly beating other guys in feats of strength and endurance. In two full seasons of high-school wrestling I won exactly two matches, one against a kid built like somebody's chubby kid sister and the other against a guy so badly affected by teenage growth spurts gone awry that he basically tripped over his disproportionately large feet and pinned himself.

Anyway, the cop's Dodge easily ran down my Monte Carlo, especially amazing given the head start I had on it. Nevertheless, I continued blowing through red lights, my work boot mashing the throttle to the floor, as I tried to stretch out some distance. It was late December, freezing cold and it had just snowed.

After barely a half-mile of wringing out the anemic 305 cu.in. V-8 in my Monte Carlo, my charge was slowed at an intersection blocked by a snowplow truck and a car stopped for a red light. I hit the brakes and swerved down a side street. By then, though, the cop was glued to my back end like a bumper sticker. At this point in the "chase" he'd undoubtedly memorized my license plate number, radioed for backup and called home to tell his wife he was going to be late for dinner. I knew this at the time, but all of the adrenaline had triggered some kind of reptilian flight mechanism in my tiny brain and I couldn't make myself stop.

From the back seat my cousin's friend, undoubtedly (and rightfully) fearing for his life, was trying to reason with the half-wit behind the wheel. "MICHAEL, CALM DOWN," he said, not exactly yelling, but urging in a strong authoritarian voice that I'm sure his father must have also used whenever dealing with hysterical nutcases as a State Trooper. "JUST CALM DOWN AND PULL OVER."

"I'VE GOT TO KEEP RUNNING!" the primitive swamp dweller now in charge of my body replied.

"GOT TO RUN!"

I rounded a corner and headed back toward Central Avenue via an ice-slicked parking lot where the local Dodge dealer parked surplus inventory. I slipped and slid sloppily across the parking lot half out of control and then, without stopping, drove out into a rush of oncoming traffic, hoping to deftly slip in among the stream of automobiles. Instead, I clumsily smashed into the front fender of a passing car.

The soundtrack of a car wreck is sickening, unmistakable and unforgettable First there's the impact: POW! Then there's the goosebump-raising squeal of metal-to-metal friction accompanied by the tinkling sound of broken glass. I remember seeing my Monte Carlo's plastic grill floating through the air, spinning end over end then watching it bounce off the pavement as I tried to veer away from the car I'd hit.

Apparently the impact shocked the reasonable side of my brain back into operation and, fearing that I'd hurt an innocent motorist, I pulled into the parking lot of a nearby restaurant. The cop swaggered up to the car with reckless abandon, threw open the door with one hand and pulled me out of the car with the other. For added effect, he then reached in, grabbed the keys out of the ignition and threw them across the hood of the car.

"Ride's over!" he said, shoving me down to the hood of my Monte Carlo and slapping on the handcuffs. He then locked me in the back seat of the police car and headed over to the accident. By then, no less than six patrol cars were on the scene. Bits and pieces of plastic and glass were strewn all over Central Avenue and I could see the owner of the car I had hit, staring at the carnage with a glassy, dazed expression.

When the cop returned to fill out an accident report, I choked up the nerve to ask about the people riding in the car I'd slammed into.

"Are they all right?"

"They've probably been better," he said.

"Are they hurt?"

"No, they're OK. You're lucky."

"I know."

A few minutes later I was locked, handcuffed in the back of a police van en route to the Albany police department's downtown building. I was seated in a room where a bunch of cops were working at desks. The cop who had arrested me was there, wildly writing tickets. Another, seated at a desk facing me, came over and removed the cuffs.

"We're not holding you," he said. "Do you live at home with your parents?"

I nodded affirmatively.

"Give me the phone number... I'll call them."

I gave him my parents' number and just sat there scared witless as he spoke to what I figured must've been my father. I knew my parents had probably already heard I had been taken away in cuffs. When I last saw my cousin and his friend, they were still standing at the accident scene. The cops towed my car away to an impound lot, leaving them without a ride home. Apparently, they used a nearby pay phone to call my uncle (my father's younger brother) for a ride. He immediately called my father.

"Your father said he'd be here just as soon as he could find a big enough baseball bat to whack you with," the cop told me, chuckling as he hung up the phone. (**Note:** In reading an early draft of this book, my parents wanted it made clear that the cop was just kidding and that my father didn't really say he was looking for a big baseball bat. Though he should've been.)

Probably seeing that I was on the verge of blubbering like a baby, humiliating myself further, he kept speaking to me.

"Are you in school?" he asked.

"Yeah, I go to the community college."

"Do you commute?"

"Yeah. Well, I did. Back when I actually had a driver's license."

He laughed a little then offered some reassurance.

"Look... no one was hurt, you weren't drunk or high and you *had* a clean license. This isn't the end of the world and you're still going to be able to drive back and forth to school or work when this is over. It's going to cost you some money and you might have trouble getting car insurance, but it'll be OK."

I shook my head affirmatively and thanked him.

"Sheesh, you know this wouldn't have happened at all if you had just pulled over," he said. "Even if you had gotten away from the car that was chasing you, another car would've caught you. You can't get away with that kind of stuff nowadays. You can't outrun the radio."

Nice people the Albany Police, and 99 percent of police in my experience, when you're not behaving like an imbecile, making their jobs more difficult than it already is. Since my driver license was clean and I was only under the influence of low IQ at the time of the incident, my parents' lawyer was able to talk the assistant district attorney into dropping many of the charges, except those that related directly to my stupidly hitting another person's car. More than fair.

My parents cut me a lot of slack too and remained amazingly calm through the entire affair. Somehow they resisted the urge to whack me with a baseball bat.

I wonder to this day however, if in private they weren't questioning whether or not they should've ever bought me that stupid go-kart.

# Chapter 4
## There's no I in Team but there's definitely one in Idiot

No one can survive La Carrera Panamericana without the aid of some very patient, skilled and dedicated people who won't punch you in the head when you become truly annoying.

I'm lucky if I can get out of my driveway without crashing into the mailbox or change a flat tire without busting off all the wheel studs and poking an eye out with the lug wrench. So I was especially fortunate to know three guys willing to put up with me while driving from Upstate New York to the southern tip of Mexico and back.

Kim foolishly signed on first, nearly a year prior. Then my friend Ken broke down and agreed to go, after I pestered him. A few months before we took off for the race, Ken wisely recruited his old friend Scott to come along.

When I first met Kim, he wasn't an engineer in the Merchant Marines, tattooed with sea dragons and coiled snakes. He was your basic 5-foot, 10-inch, 135-pound, smart ass, grudgingly attending Ravena-Coeymans-Selkirk Central High School, circa 1984.

Like everyone else I hung around with, Kim was into cars — but not the American pushrod V-8 variety the rest of us were raised on. His thing was air-cooled Volkswagens and Porsches. Unlike me, Kim was (and is) very intelligent. I recall thinking, for instance, *Ha! It sure is fun sitting in 11th grade chemistry class with my pals making fart jokes and not memorizing this stupid Periodic Table of the Elements!* Then, at the end of the year, Kim breezed through the final exam while I laughed and fart joked all the way to summer school, so that I could still graduate on time.

Before I met Kim, we had a friend in common, Ken, whom I'd met in middle school when both of us were on the modified wrestling team. Ken and I immediately hit it off. Today, Ken is a self-employed auto mechanic and one of the most trustworthy people on the planet. I owe him a lifetime of favors including one big one: In 1988, when we were a year or so out of high school, Ken choked up the nerve to introduce himself to a couple of pretty high-school seniors named Billie Jo and Kathy, who were working at the local drug store. We all went out on our first date a couple weeks after that charming intro. All these years later, I'm still married to Kathy and he's still married to Billie Jo.

Moral to the story: Some guys are just naturally born to fix-up stuff. Cars, people, whatever, Ken can figure out how to make it all work.

By our senior year in high school, Ken, Kim and I were by and large inseparable. We wiled away the sleepy 1950s-like Reagan-era much the way my Dad wiled away the original 1950s — thinking we should be worried about nuclear war with the Russians, jabbering about and illegally street racing cars and burning up all the cheap gas our crappy after-school part-time jobs would buy.

We were three average kids, products of blue-collar households, complete with a textbook case of

1950s American middle-class values and work ethics growing up in a gritty rural/industrial town. Saturday nights we'd either head to Central Avenue in Albany looking for trouble or just line Ken's 1973 Mustang up against my 1969 Camaro on an infrequently traveled stretch of country road. Kim would fearlessly stand between the two cars and flag us off, then we would run door handle to door handle on a roughly marked out quarter-mile.

Out of hundreds of passes, I could count on one hand the number of times I managed to beat Ken in a drag race. He was always screwing around with his Mustang: changing gear ratios, switching from an automatic transmission to a four-speed, swapping engines etc. Meanwhile I'd just show up with the same stupid old car, hoping Ken would accidentally stick the shifter in reverse or maybe one of his wheels would fall off or something.

It took me at least a month of careful huckstering to get Ken to agree to leave his wife and kids behind, not to mention take two full weeks off from his self-made auto repair business to go with Kim and I to Mexico for the Carrera. At some point in my delirium about competing in the race, I actually imagined driv-

One of the few times Ken's Mustang wasn't five or six car lengths ahead of my Camaro was when we parked to have this photo taken at our high-school graduation in 1987.

— PHOTO BY BOB MUELLER

ing the race car the entire 7,000 miles. It sounded very cool and maybe it's possible, but having a truck pulling a trailer (neither of which we actually had yet) and Ken to drive it would ease some of the pressure.

Prior to enlisting Ken's help for our team, I had also enlisted the help of a friend named Steve whom I'd met covering a story for the *Times Union*. Steve arranged to send a group of area high-school students on the Great Race — an annual vintage cross-country road rally for antique and classic cars. He got them a Model A Ford racer to drive, as well as a truck and a trailer, plus he helped raise support money from sponsors, generated publicity for the effort and more, all through his own not-for-profit organization.

For our effort, Steve graciously rounded up a 24-foot enclosed trailer from a friend. He even paid to have the brakes and wheel bearings freshened and performed some much needed sheetmetal repairs to the outside of the trailer. No strings attached, no charge.

I also made it a point to heckle Gerie Bledsoe, a racer who devoted considerable time and resources to not only competing quite seriously in the Carrera but, at the time, served as the point man for other competitors. (Gerie has since retired from that role, but still coordinates another rally event, the Chihuahua Express. For more about that head to www.chihuahuaexpress.com.)

I buried poor Gerie under an avalanche of emails full of dumb questions because, not only is he knowledgeable about the Carrera, but he'd won the class in which we would be competing. Gerie dealt with each question seriously and promptly, without ever once threatening to file for a restraining order against me.

One of the greatest favors that Gerie did for me was introduce me to Jose Rubio — a Carrera veteran from Mexico who took pity on our pathetic effort and took us completely under wing. More about Jose, his big, friendly, Mexican co-pilot Hugo as well as his wife, brother-in-law and sister, later.

While I was team building, my always-enterprising friend Ken had begun doing the very same thing.

One night, out for dinner, Ken told me that he wanted to make the trip to Mexico a foursome.

"I told my buddy Scott about the trip and he thought it sounded cool," Ken said.

I knew Scott only through Ken, but my impression was that he was quiet, hardworking, good at making stuff go when it really doesn't want to and he liked to travel in his dual-wheel pickup pulling a giant fifth-wheel camper trailer.

In other words, he was perfect.

Plus, having two guys driving the truck and trailer in an unfamiliar country was a lot safer and smarter than just one, since Kim and I would have our hands full with the race.

Suddenly our team was, well, a team. At the time, I hoped that we would work together well enough to make it down to the Carrera and back without incident. And at the very least, I wanted all of these guys still speaking to me when we rolled back into town.

# Chapter 5

## Uh, no thanks... just looking

---

**L**ate in the summer of 2003, before we told more than just a handful of people we were serious about the Carrera, Kim and I started hunting for a race car. The Carrera's rulebook called for a machine of 1965-vintage or older, which allowed for dozens of possibilities. Kim said he was begging off on the actual shopping, though he'd be happy to go take a look at anything I was interested in buying. As a compulsive car shopper, this was OK with me.

Even as I write this on my computer, I've got a web browser running in the background, tuned into some pile of untapped potential for sale on the internet.

The truth is, though, I don't really like buying. I like browsing. Buying just means that the search is over and I have to haul something home and figure out what to do with it. Invariably this will lead to spending more money. But browsing never has to end and it doesn't cost anything.

I guess what scares me the most about car buying is that over the course of a dozen or so vehicle transactions, I have yet to sell a car or truck for more than I have invested. I think it's because I was raised Catholic, so I think I'll burn in eternal hellfire for pricing my own stuff too high and feeling like I ripped someone off. I call it being "realistic" and "honest." But, if I had to trade on the value of cars and trucks for a living, I'd call it, "going bankrupt."

Since the pre-1965 car Kim and I were shopping for would end up a race car, there wasn't much sense even pretending that we could recoup the money we were going to spend on it. Race cars will burn through your hard earned cash like a Ponzi scheme, all on the promise of some glamorous, exciting future. Still, I dreamed about buying a valuable car at a bargain price, then using elbow grease and ingenuity to get it race ready. Afterward I'd sell it and recoup everything. Maybe there'd even be a profit. (Ha!)

Our first old-car shopping trip took us to what should've probably been the final resting place of an old Mustang in Western Vermont.

The Mustang is a no-brainer as a Carrera car. Small, light and easy to turn into a racer, thanks to the fact that Ford pumped out 50 bazillion of them and there are literally dozens companies who do nothing but deal in parts for every vintage Mustang.

There are monthly magazines specifically about Mustangs, classified books with huge sections devoted to all manners of Mustangs and Mustang-related parts. The internet is full of Mustang information.

I found the aforementioned Mustang in one of the local car trader rags. A 1965 coupe, in pieces and stripped, but in good, basic shape, the ad promised. Best of all it could be had for less than $2,000.

"It needs a lot of work," the owner told me over the phone. "But it's basically solid and it comes with a convertible parts car."

Kim was home from sailing the high seas for a few months, so I talked him into going for a look. We pulled in the driveway and the seller, a young guy, his young wife and their toddler kids were all outside. The Mustang was alongside the driveway, and a quick inspection revealed that the floors and trunk were badly rusted while most of the exterior sheetmetal had been hastily patched and painted at some point, probably years prior.

When new, 1960s and 1970s American pony cars were shoddily built with the crush resistance of a cheese puff. Add some aggressive, strategically located rust to the mix and you've got yourself a metal fatigued, crack-prone coffin. With big smiles, we politely thanked the guy and his wife and kids for wasting our time and moved on.

Our next stop was a few weeks later at the home of a 1957 Lincoln Capri two-door in Western New York. Admittedly this wasn't one of my best ideas, but the Lincoln looked so cool on eBay with its frazzled '50s pink paint, (Lincoln called the color Flamingo that year, I believe) those shark-like fins and scowling grill.

The owner had amassed about a dozen old cars and squirreled them away in garages all around his town, but the cabin-cruiser sized Lincoln was huddled down like a big pink earthworm in his backyard. The body wasn't bad, but the springs were probably clapped —

This 1957 Lincoln we found on eBay was really nice, but engine and chassis parts for these cars can be pricy. Pink wouldn't have been our first color choice for a race car either.

possibly from just trying to support the 4,000-pound car while sitting parked for decades. Its interior was surprisingly intact and still had plastic covers on the seats, though everything was crusty from neglect. To our surprise, its 368-cubic-inch V-8 fired off with a healthy roar and the automatic transmission responded when shifted into gear. It was a cool car — ripe for customization and it would've made a nice cruiser.

The owner pressed us to make a deal, but the Lincoln was too much automobile for us. It wasn't in bad condition and would've made a unique entrant in the Carrera. But with questionable parts availability, probably at a premium prices, we decided to beg off.

Next, I talked Kim into taking a quick trip down to South Carolina to check out a 1956 Chevrolet two-door — basically just a body and frame that I found on the internet. The seller said its floors, frame and trunk were solid and the price was in our range.

It took us about 12 hours to drive to the guy's place. When we arrived, I looked around for the '56 with solid floors and trunk that he'd advertised. There was one car parked near the entrance to his fenced-in junkyard that sort of matched the description and vaguely looked like the car in the photos.

The seller turned out to be a tall, gangly guy, in need of a shower and a clean set of clothes.

"I called yesterday about the '56 that you have for sale. Where is it?" I asked him.

A 24-hour drive to South Carolina and back to look at a 1956 Chevrolet turned out to be a waste of time. That car isn't in this photo, this is just a representative sample of the seller's clean, one-owner inventory at the time.

He pointed one of his long greasy fingers in the direction of the car I had hoped wasn't the one we had driven 12 hours to look at.

"The floors are solid and I have some pieces you could use to fix the trunk," he told me with a straight face.

I pulled open the trunk lid and stared at the South Carolina soil through the holes in the floor. I paced around the car's tattered corpse, wondering just what the hell I had been thinking. Nothing about the car was worth saving — what wasn't rusted had been amateurishly repaired a few years before Kim and I were born. The "solid" floors were as thin as coffee filters — I didn't bother to peer underneath at the frame rails. It was a complete pile and I wanted to punch the seller in the face.

Kim didn't even bother to walk over and look at the '56. Instead, he was already poking around in the field that surrounded the seller's barn looking at the other junk cars. At this point, he must've thought I was completely insane. I know I sure as hell did. Kim's a trouper though and he never complained. After we left the graveyard of old Chevrolets he insisted on stopping at a convenience store, picking up a book of old cars for sale (this was 2003, before smart phones and craigslist) and hunting up some other possibilities. I was tired of looking at basket cases though and floored it for Upstate New York.

Over the ensuing weeks, I continued to scour the want ads looking for a car. Frankly, I was starting to feel a little pinched—it was late summer 2003 and we wanted to race in the following year's Carrera, which would kick off in October 2004.

That meant buying a car, doing the chassis work,

installing a roll cage, building or buying a suitable drivetrain, brakes, wiring, interior, etc. The thing is, I'm an O.K. shade-tree mechanic and I'm fairly ambitious. For some people, prepping a car for this race would be no biggie. For me, it was going to be like launching a monkey into outer space.

Of course, it was Mr. Fix-it-Upper Ken who found the car — a 1961 Impala two-door hardtop. I had noticed it languishing in the local classifieds, and judging by the phone number knew it was less than five miles down the road. I liked the fact that it was listed as having a four-speed transmission and a Chevrolet 348-cu.in. V-8 engine, the forerunner to the more famous 409. But at $7,000-plus, the price was so high, I never bothered to call about it.

Ken, however, had heard other things about the car's price among the whisperings of local gear heads. The story was that the owner was looking to move the car. Reasonable offers would be met with a hand-shake and ownership papers.

So, a little nervous with anticipation, I made the call and arranged an appointment.

The Impala, Roman Red and white, sat neglected and unwanted like a pile of dirty laundry in the back of the owner's garage.

It was tattered but looked like a museum piece compared to all of the other junk Kim and I had looked at. Plus, sure enough, it was already a four-speed manual, had a big, old Chevrolet 348 V-8 under the hood and it was a two-door hardtop (a roofline that enthusiasts refer to as a "bubble top") — all definite selling points.

The quarters and lower portions of the doors had been poorly patched with body filler and there was a fist-sized hole in the passenger's side rocker panel. However, its red paint, though cracked and weathered, was largely intact and the interior sported a funky tuck-and-roll job with red Chevy bowties sewn into the backrests.

I knew this was the car and offered the seller $5,000, figuring I could always unload it for that kind of money, running or not. He jumped at the chance to get rid of the Impala and even said he'd deliver it. It was a good deal and besides, all of this browsing had worn even me out.

I was eager to get building a race car and I knew this old dinosaur was substantial enough to cart us safely across Mexico and simple enough to repair when the need arose.

# Chapter 6
## Car? Yes. Race car? Hmmm

It was a hot August night when the Impala was scheduled to make its debut at the McNessor residence and I was busy preparing for its arrival by pacing around and looking out the window every three minutes. Trading perfectly good money for a car always makes me anxious, especially when the car is a sagging, wheezing and faded 1961 Chevrolet, that I had about a year to make durable enough for the Carrera.

The guy who delivered the Impala eased it off the trailer and into my garage under its own power. The old, el cheapo dual-exhaust system let out a familiar high-school parking lot hot rod rumble, but the big 348 engine had a noticeable skip—like a bad valve or a lifter.

It didn't matter. All of that stuff, the exhaust, the 348, etc. would have to come out anyway—even though at the time I was deluding myself into believing that some of the car's components might be workable.

Kim showed up for a look a couple of hours later. Though he definitely would've preferred an air-cooled German sports car to the Impala, he seemed satisfied that we finally owned the race car we would ride to glory in the Great Mexican Road Race.

For me, it couldn't get any cooler than a 1961 Impala, two-door hardtop with the 348, four-speed combination. The McNessor clan has a long proud history of Impala stewardship, though this would be my first brush with the Big Car. A couple of Camaros. Several Chevy pickups. A Monte Carlo. All excellent, dirt reliable, vehicles. But never Chevrolet's plus-sized model.

New car dealerships today are crammed with vehicles outfitted for every conceivable purpose and self image: All-wheel-drive compacts with hybrid power-

The unsuspecting Impala about a day or so after its arrival at Chez McNessor. It had still had no clue about the indignities and abuse that lie ahead.

trains; Nine passenger front-wheel-drive vans with built-in wifi hot spots; Six-hundred horsepower retro-themed muscle cars that will run a 12-second quarter, while the driver reclines in a 12-way power adjustable heated and cooled seat; Towering pickup trucks rolling on 35-inch off-road tires with suspension like a Baja 1000 prerunner — perfect for hopping curbs in the mall parking lot.

Meanwhile, Impalas built in the last 20 years are about as exciting as treating yourself to the tuna casserole early bird special after a day spent binge watching Matlock. Big family cars used to be the red meat of Detroit's diet. Now they're a side order of steamed cauliflower — consumed out of an obligation to make the sensible choice.

In 1958, when the Impala made its debut as the top-of-the-line model, Chevrolet basically sold two cars: the Corvette and a full-size car, in a few different body types — coupe, sedan, convertible, four-door, station wagon etc. — with a few different model names — Impala, Bel Air, Biscayne.

Trucks, which have become the defacto family car today, were purely for work, not guys who actually need a four-door family car but feel more macho in a pickup.

Buying a performance car, other than the Corvette, meant ordering a Chevrolet car with the biggest engine available — the 348, until late 1961 when the 409 arrived.

The design of 1959 and 1960 full-size Chevrolet cars is usually said to have been influenced by early jet aircraft. But everything on an aircraft is designed for a purpose. The '59 and '60 Chevys were just built to look flamboyant and showy, like a prop in one of Liberace's Vegas shows.

The A-pillar in fact was so heavily "styled" that Chevrolet had to print up a set of step-by-step instructions showing how to get in the car without knocking the fedora off your Brylcreemed head.

For '61, the design was similar to the '60 but just a little less fabulous. Still, the Jet Age styling cues were evident: the big, bubble-shaped greenhouse on the two-door hardtop was reminiscent of the cockpit canopy of an F-86 fighter jet; the painted swoosh and spear-shaped trim on the side was meant to look like a jet vapor trail; and the bullet shaped taillights resembled lit afterburners.

I didn't know any of this the first time I saw a 1961

Impala. On a Sunday in the late 1970s, my Dad took me to Lebanon Valley Dragway to watch the races. One of the local guys was running a white '61 Impala. When it left the line it looked like a Korean War era fighter plane blasting off the deck of an aircraft carrier — front end high, rear crouched low to the ground, its big-block engine howling.

It reminded me of the car in a photograph in my Mother's photo album. A picture of my Dad. He was a young man, about age 20, with his whole life ahead of him. He wore a proud smile and was leaning against his brand new white, 1960 Impala with a 348 and three carburetors — one of the hottest production cars of its day.

In 1965, my Dad stepped up to the first car I ever rode in: a 1965 Impala SS with the then-new Mark IV big-block 396 engine and a four-speed. Silver on the outside, black bucket seat interior inside.

It was more than 50 years ago that he took delivery of that car, but to this day, when my old man talks about his 1965 Impala SS, it's like he's 25 again, working every second of overtime he could as a welder at the cement plant in order to support a growing family, eventually start his own trucking business and make

My old man and his brand-new 1960 Impala, powered by
a 348 with three two-barrel carburetors. It was this picture that warped my view of automobiles and probably
led me to choose a 1961 Impala with the big 348 to race
in La Carrera Panamericana. Unfortunately all those
years I looked at his proud smile in my Mom's photo
album, I had no idea he was thinking: *This is the worst
handling automobile I've ever driven.*

the payments on a brand-new '65 Impala SS.

I was two when that car was sold to raise the proceeds for a new Chevelle and a new Chevy pickup, yet I know more about his street racing exploits in the Impala than I know about my own.

The '65 Impala was a departure from the 1958-'64 X-frame cars and when my father stepped into the dealership to place his order, he knew it. For starters, it was built on a perimeter-type "Girder-Guard" frame sturdy enough to serve as a railroad overpass. Plus, the front and rear suspension, as well as the steering of the '65, were all new, which made the Impala handle more like a modern car and less like a runaway river barge.

The 409 engine was still available in 1965, but the old man was having no part of that. He wanted the all-new 396 Mark IV big-block engine with its "porcupine" canted-valve, wedge heads. The salesman who sold him the car knew nothing about the Mark IV so the old man had to educate him about the 396s mid-year availability.

My father wasn't the only person to trade a portion of his hard-earned paycheck for a new Impala in 1965. Chevrolet sold 56,600 six-cylinder Impalas and

746,800 V-8 cars (including Caprice and station wagons) for a grand total of 803,400 cars. It sold 243,114 Impalas with the Super Sport option. Incredible.

That '65 ruined my father for earlier Impalas and these days, he doesn't really share his son's affection for Chevy's 1958-'64 X-frame cars ("worst-handling cars ever") or 348/409 W engines ("boat anchors"). He rarely talks about his '60 Impala and regards the scruffy '61 two-door hardtop that took up residency at my place as an old beater. But when I look at it, I'm 10 years old, watching that white '61 devouring the quarter mile at Lebanon Valley Dragway.

In my father's defense, the X-frame Chevrolets were a product of their time. They were about as safe as everything else in the 1960s: leaded gas, smoking cigarettes on airplanes; ducking and covering under a desk in the event of a nuclear attack. Most people assume that a big old American car like the '61 Impala would somehow fare better in a crash than a modern compact car.

But old cars had all the crush resistance of a Lucky Strike, they had solid steering columns that would skewer the driver like a barbecued shrimp in the event of a crash and metal dashboards built to withstand a high-speed impact with a fragile human skull.

Today, the 348/409 engine is popular with the nostalgia crowd, but it's one of Chevrolet's clunkier post war V-8 engine designs. For its displacement, the 348 is big and heavy: about 650 pounds compared to 575 pounds for a small block 350. The W engine's combustion-chamber-in-block design had some manufacturing advantages but was no Hemi in terms of moving intake and exhaust gases in and out. It sure was cool looking though, with those scalloped heads, especially when topped with chrome valve covers and a multi-carburetor intake.

All that said, it seems like I couldn't have picked a worse car than a 1961 Impala to enter in La Carrera Panamericana. Wrong. Sure, the Impala was ill handling, hard stopping, unsafe and powered by a big, heavy, obsolete V-8 engine. But to my inner 10-year old, it looked like the fastest car on the planet.

# Chapter 7
## Building the imperfect beast

**F**irst I insured and registered the Impala, so I could drive it legally down the road and determine if it was even close to being ready to run in a 1,700-mile Mexican road rally. Big surprise, it wasn't.

I'm a professional automotive journalist so, in keeping with tradition, instead of actually doing anything, I decided to write a critique of the good and bad things about the car.

On the bad side:

- It leaned over so far in the turns that it practically scraped the rain gutters on the pavement. A quick roadside inspection revealed that the spindly front swaybar was disconnected. Problem number one solved. (Hey, this was going to be a lot easier than I thought!)

- The steering was loose. Scary loose. Like some important parts under there in the dark weren't hooked to anything anymore kind of loose.
- Operating the old tattered-looking Hurst shifter was like stirring a bucket of roofing tar mid-February in upstate New York.
- The 348 seemed to be making slightly more horsepower and considerably less torque than the rototiller engine in my old go kart.
- The springs, front and rear, were sacked as badly as those in the '57 Lincoln I'd considered buying for about three ill-advised seconds.
- The headlights worked, provided the high beams were switched on and then only the center two glowed. Dimly. Half of the taillights and brake lights worked. But the turn signals on each side flashed intermittently, like the red signal lights on a railroad crossing. A couple of the lenses had been smashed out too.
- The windshield wiper motor made only a grunt-

ing noise when the switch was turned on — a feat that required Herculean thumb and forefinger strength because the knob was missing.

- The floor of the trunk was pretty rusted and in need of replacement, as was the passenger's side rocker panel.
- It was running a points-type distributor and a generator. Those would have to be replaced with a modern alternator and a breakerless ignition.

On the good side:

- The brakes worked, but most of the antiquated system would have to be pulled off and thrown away for safety's sake. Some of the lines looked homemade and the master cylinder was of the old one-pot variety. This means if you lose part of your brakes, you lose all of your brakes and barrel roll off the side of 9,000-foot-high inactive volcano cone in Mexico.
- The tires were pretty good, though they were wimpy narrow white walls.

The tic, tic, tic, skip, skip, skipping from the engine was grating on me the most, so I yanked off the valve covers for a look. The rocker arms were moving but they were all over the place in terms of adjustment.

Someone had obviously been in there monkeying around before me trying to make the 348 sound a little more healthy. The plug wires and cap were new as well. Undoubtedly someone had changed them hoping they were the cause of the skip. More likely it was a bent valve, or a bad lifter.

It didn't really matter. There was just no way that this 650-pound, 348 cubic-inch slug was up to a 1,700-mile thrash across Mexico, anyway. However, I couldn't really yank the engine until I had solved about a dozen other problems. By that time, Kim was out at sea working. It was September, the mercury was dropping and I was starting to feel the pressure of having a lot of work to do while not being completely sure how to do any of it.

So, like anybody with more credit than brains, I took out my Visa card and started wildly ordering parts. While waiting for the boxes to start arriving, I built myself a sturdy new workbench out of scrap lumber that had been lying around since we finished building our house the year prior, figuring I'd need it. (The workbench actually earned me more compliments than my work on the Impala.) I decided to take on the jobs I felt most comfortable with: replacing the floor in the trunk and rebuilding the front suspension. The trunk was fairly easy. One evening after work, I snipped out the old floor and then over the two following nights, tacked in a ready-made panel purchased from an aftermarket parts outfit. It looked pretty good and it gave me some confidence. Though I never did actually finish the job. As you read this, the new floor is still unpainted.

I then decided to tackle the loose front end. Following Ken's advice, I snipped out the old coil springs with the torch. A couple of quick cuts and out the rusted old steel curls came in a few useless pieces. Just to make sure I would have all of the fingers I would later need to write this book, I wrapped a chain around the springs first, preventing the pieces from flying. I've replaced coil springs before, but all of that kinetic energy yearning to be free has always spooked me.

With the springs out, I then sledge hammered the rest of the 40-something-year-old parts out of the car until I was left with just a bare frame. While lying on my back staring up at the Impala's old bones, I noticed that in the process of transporting the car at some point in its life, someone had hooked a chain

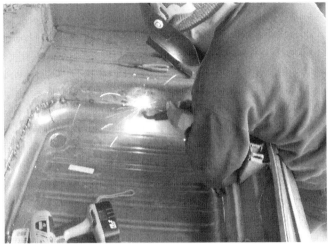

Above: Tacking in a reproduction trunk floor. Below, driving out the old control arm bushings with a socket and long extension, rather than the correct tool for the job.

in one of the factory holes in the frame and then yearned down on it with a binder using enough force to tear the hole open several inches. This was the case in several areas, all of which would have to be repaired before the car was put back together.

Over the next month or so, working nights and weekends, I cleaned repaired, repainted and rebuilt the Impala's front end and steering mechanisms. It was dirty, mindless, knuckle-busting work. When it was finished, my hands looked like I had given myself a manicure with an ice pick and then painted my nails with satin-black chassis paint. Also, the front of the car sat *way* too high — like the repaired trunk was loaded with the crushing weight of all my worries and doubts. Or like the '61 Impala I'd seen as a kid launching off the starting line at Lebanon Valley Dragway. Only this Impala was now frozen in a sort of perpetual pounce, like a dead cat stuffed by a taxidermist. I'd of course gotten a deal I couldn't refuse on the front coil springs at a local spring shop.

"You aren't going to believe this," the guy told me over the phone, "I've got a set of those in stock."

I drove over after work and the guy behind the counter produced a cardboard box that looked like the original packaging for Abraham Lincoln's stove pipe hat. Inside was a set of coils that hadn't seen the light of day since JFK was diddling Marilyn Monroe.

"It says they're for a car with a 348 and air conditioning, so if yours doesn't have A/C they might be a little stiffer than standard springs," he said.

"How much?" I asked.

"How's $25 sound?"

"Perfect," I said, reaching into my pocket for the cash. For that price they could've been on fire and I would've grabbed them. Besides, how much difference could air conditioning make? Answer: about two inches.

Other than the weird new stance, the work I'd done under the car looked great, even though for all of my trouble it still handled like a stock 1961 Impala with manual steering.

At times, when beating apart crusty old front end pieces with a hammer and chisel was more fun than I could stand, I would jump over to other tasks. Like the ignition, for instance, or the underhood wiring, exhaust and fuel systems.

I decided to tackle all of this stuff before I removed the old engine because:

A) I was scared that if I ripped the entire car apart at once, I would forget how to put it back together and eventually wind up just carting off the individual pieces to the scrap yard someday after Kim had stopped speaking to me for good.

B) I justified the previous reason by telling myself I should tackle all of these other jobs one by one and then test each improvement with the current engine. If everything worked with the old engine, it should work with the new one as well.

# Chapter 8
## Gasoline? We don't need no stinking gasoline!

True confession. I used to have an irrational fear of carburetors. Like my other irrational fears, it started when I was young, growing up in the 1970s: Guys in heavy makeup like Bozo the Clown or Gene Simmons of KISS; getting hit in the head by falling parts of SkyLab; or a great white shark attacking me in the town swimming pool.

I was about 11 and the engine in my 1978 Suzuki DS100 dirt bike was running funny, so I just guessed it was something to do with the carburetor. In retrospect, the pilot jet was probably a little bit clogged causing it to run lean off idle and hesitate when you hit (or "blip") the throttle.

The repair is so simple on a Mikuni carburetor that a child slightly smarter than I was at the time could do it: 1.) Flip the carburetor over; 2.) Remove the four screws that secure the float bowl; 3.) Remove the pilot jet and clean the gunk out of the little holes that get clogged up with dirt, because after all it's a *dirt* bike. 4.) Put the jet back in, put the float bowl back on, then go try and break your stupid little neck dirt biking.

That earlier version of me would not learn all of this until later in life, however. When I was a kid, there was no internet on which to find an exploded-view diagram of a Mikuni carburetor or look up videos of people having sex. You also couldn't snap pictures of things with your smart phone as you took them apart to refer to when you tried to put said things back together. Phones back then were one of the few things dumber than me.

Sure, there were shop manuals, but I didn't have the money to buy one. And if I was going to take step-by-step photos of the carburetor coming apart, it would've meant, borrowing my mother's Kodak Instamatic, hoping there were enough exposures on the roll leftover from my sister's First Communion, mailing off the film and then waiting however long it took for the pictures to arrive from Rochester, N.Y.

I didn't have time for any of that. I needed to get my Suzuki running properly so I could go and try breaking my stupid little neck as quickly as possible.

Well, just to make this story brief and far less painful for you than it has been for me, when I took the carburetor apart, the needle somehow dropped out of its seat and I inadvertently kicked it under the workbench. After cleaning everything, I put it back together, not knowing that the needle was missing, and when I turned the fuel on, gasoline ran unchecked out of every orifice in the carburetor.

I assumed I'd ruined the carburetor, so I stopped riding the bike. When I'd saved enough money — earned helping my father work on his dump trucks (he paid me $1 an hour if I kept the money or $2 if I promised to put it in the bank) or cleaning out a dead lady's house — I plunked down $54 on a brand new 24 mm Mikuni. This was not an insignificant amount of money for an 11-year-old kid making $1 an hour and it amounted to almost 20 percent of the purchase price of the bike.

The guy at the motorcycle shop who ordered the carburetor tried to talk some sense into me, like a bartender serving a drunk his fourth round of shots.

"You know, there really isn't much that can go wrong with those carburetors. Why don't you bring it in and we'll take a look at it. It's probably an easy fix."

But I was so ashamed that I'd done something so incredibly stupid, that I talked the guy out of selling me a 60-cent needle, saving me about $53 dollars.

Years later, when my parents were moving and we were cleaning out my father's garage, I found the Mikuni box with the old carburetor inside stashed in a drawer under the bench where he used to let me work. Just for kicks, I pulled off the float bowl. Immediately I noticed there was no needle in the seat. I pulled the bench away from the wall and there on the ground underneath it, was the needle.

These days, I'm no longer afraid of carburetors. You can't help but admire the way these Rube Goldberg contraptions can turn liquid fuel into a fine mist, continuously feeding the fires of an internal combustion engine.

But when I was putting the Impala together I still wasn't totally comfortable with carburetors and I figured that the Carerra's altitude changes would require jetting adjustments on the fly — something I definitely wasn't comfortable with.

One day while looking over the race rulebook I noticed a one-sentence passage stating that competitors were permitted to use an approved Liquified Petroleum Gas fuel system.

Up to that point, my experience using LPG, or propane as it's often referred to, was limited to burning steaks and burgers on the grill and using the gas to fuel a little heater in my garage to ward off winter's icy grip.

I was surprised to learn that LPG is recognized by the federal Environmental Protection Agency as a clean fuel and that exhaust from propane-fueled vehicles contains 60 percent less carbon monoxide than exhaust from comparable gasoline fueled vehicles. And because the fuel systems are sealed, there are no evaporative emissions to worry about, as there are with older gasoline-fueled vehicles.

LPG generally has a higher octane rating than gasoline, making it possible to run higher compression—the stuff in the bottle under your gas grill is probably 104 octane — and because LPG enters the engine as a gas sucked in by engine vacuum, rather than being pumped in as a liquid at a constant rate, LPG systems adapt easily to conditions that befuddle a gasoline carburetor.

After reading what specific information I could find about LPG vehicle conversions on the internet, I emailed a guy who handles LPG fuel systems, for a major engine rebuilding company, to buy some parts.

He quoted me some new prices for the pieces I'd need, which were substantially higher than what I could afford. He also advised against running a dedicated LPG system, pushing instead a "dual-fuel" system that would allow me to run either gasoline or LPG. His concern was that I might find myself out of fuel without access to an LPG filling station. A valid point, but a dual-fuel system would've been twice as complicated, twice as expensive and twice as heavy. Dual-fuel systems also don't perform quite as well as dedicated LPG-only systems and they require the use of a carburetor which I was afraid of at the time.

With my knowledge of LPG fuel systems still fairly sketchy, I began scouring the internet for cheap used parts. Just before Christmas, I located two complete

The used Impco 450 cfm mixer that would replace the Impala's carburetor is the tall thing pictured top left. To the right of the mixer is a vacuum operated fuel shutoff and on the bottom right, next to the bottle of Simple Green, is the LPG converter. That gets plumbed into the engine's coolant and the warm coolant from the engine heats the LPG, turning it into a gas. It's remarkably simple to understand, even for a guy whose afraid of carburetors, and I bought two complete systems on eBay for $50 each.

systems that I figured would work on the Impala's 348 engine, minus the propane fuel tank and the fuel line. I had no idea if the parts were in working condition and the description noted that they were completely covered with a thick layer of grime. At 50 bucks each, I figured it was worth the risk so I bought both sets for $100 hoping that I could cobble together one functioning system.

When the parts arrived they were indeed filthy, but from what little I knew, they weren't broken or worn out. I picked what looked to be the best pieces out of the pile and proceeded to wash them up in the garage sink.

By handling them and eyeballing them, I started to piece together how they probably worked. Everything seemed really simple, which it would have to be if I was ever going to make it work. The other problem was, I still didn't have an LPG fuel tank designed for a vehicle. Nevertheless, I got busy making brackets to mount the LPG converter and the fuel lock-off valve and shopping for a carb adapter that would allow me to bolt the LPG mixer to the 348's original cast-iron manifold.

By February, I had the stuff in the engine compartment installed and began looking for a fuel tank. I found a tank in new condition on the internet that was virtually the perfect size for the Impala's trunk. It was mine for a mere $175 — about half what these tanks cost new. The tank was at a nice home on the outskirts of Philadelphia — a five- to six-hour ride

The vehicle LPG tank I scored on eBay for $175 was practically brand new. It looked big enough to supply an entire RV park, but the Impala's trunk swallowed it easily.

from Albany. That week I was fortunate enough to be reviewing a new SUV for my job at the newspaper which, with the passenger's seats folded flat and a lot of blankets to make sure nothing got scratched, was just the right size to haul home the tank.

With the half-full tank safely in my garage I loaded it in the trunk of the car, ran about 17 feet of reinforced hose for fuel line, hit the key and of course, nothing happened. But after some fiddling, sure enough, the 348 roared to life and actually ran as good, if not slightly better, on LPG.

Some people are leery of burning LPG as a motor vehicle fuel because it's not used as prevalently as gasoline or diesel, especially in the Northeast. But the parts make a gasoline carburetor look like something Wile E. Coyote built to catch the Road Runner.

The average LPG fuel system is comprised of four main components and a couple of different types of hose.

In case you care, here's how an old-fashioned LPG system, used on carbureted engines, works: The tank stores the LPG under pressure so that it remains a liquid (Once the pressure is released it reverts to its gaseous state.) Crack open the tank's "liquid" valve and the LPG travels up the fuel line to a safety valve/filter in the engine compartment. This valve is operated by vacuum so, as soon as it detects a vacuum signal from the engine, it opens, sending the LPG onto the next part, called the converter.

The converter is essentially a pair of round chambers stacked on top of each other. In the rear chamber, water warmed by the engine flows through, warming the body of the converter. The LPG hits the warm converter and turns into a vapor or gas. At the bottom of the converter's gas chamber is a valve that opens when it detects engine vacuum.

The last part of the system is the mixer, which sits where the carburetor normally sits — on top of the engine's intake manifold. The mixer is connected to the converter by a long vapor hose. Inside the mixer is a rubber diaphragm and at the bottom are standard butterfly valves, like every carburetor has. When you hit the throttle and ask for fuel, the mixer sucks LPG vapor over the vapor hose from the converter and into the engine. If everything is hooked up correctly, your engine gets a whiff of LPG gas and goes, vroom, vroom.

LPG is a byproduct of crude oil refining and natural gas processing, so it obviously isn't any answer to the world's dependence on fossil fuel. However, from an air-quality perspective, LPG has some benefits. Or so I learned from an organization called the Propane Education and Research Council, that I'm sure wouldn't lie to me just to get me to burn tractor-trailer loads of propane:

- Propane exhaust creates 60 to 70 percent fewer smog-producing hydrocarbons than gasoline.
- Compared to gasoline, propane yields 12 percent

less carbon dioxide, about 20 percent less nitrous oxide and 60 percent less carbon monoxide.

- Propane cuts emissions of toxins and carcinogens like benzene and toluene by up to 96 percent over gasoline.
- Propane has an octane rating of 104, which means a propane-fueled engine can survive with a higher compression ratio than an engine fueled on unleaded pump gasoline — the highest octane gas typically found at the pumps is 94 octane. Higher compression ratios make an engine more efficient and more powerful.

If you don't believe the Propane Education and Research Council, the U.S. Environmental Protection Agency also considers LPG a clean, alternative fuel. In fact converting your vehicle to run on LPG will qualify you for a tax credit. When I converted the Impala to LPG, I was able to deduct the cost of all of the parts I purchased off my income taxes that year.

Unfortunately, with a car built in the 21st century, the cost of the conversion to LPG probably outweighs any of the aforementioned environmental benefits.

The auto industry has dreamt up clever workarounds that have minimized the damage that burning gasoline can inflict on the environment. Unless LPG is cheaper for you to obtain than gasoline — which it isn't where I live — then it probably isn't worth the effort.

With an old carbureted car, however, you might be doing the air a favor by switching to LPG. With older engines you will also enjoy longer engine oil life when running LPG, because there won't be any contamination from the fuel as there tends to be from gasoline.

Of course, it's also a great solution if you happen to have carburetor phobias like I used to. Unfortunately, it can do nothing to protect you from guys in clown makeup or great white sharks in the town swimming pool.

# Chapter 9
## More money spent, more half-truths told

Spring always seems to take its sweet time thawing Upstate New York out of its annual deep freeze and the year we were planning to make our run at the Carrera was no different.

By the time the trees were covered in the first gauzy wisps of greenery that signify everything is going to be O.K. for another six or so months, I had:

- Rejuvenated the Impala's suspension and steering;
- Installed a new wiring harness;
- Updated the antiquated charging and ignition systems with state-of-the-art mid-1970s General Motors technology;

- Bolted in a new high-torque mini starter;
- Replaced the battery and cables;
- Welded in a new trunk pan;
- Sorted out my freshly rebuilt junkyard propane fuel system; and
- Installed all new brake lines and fitted the car with an obnoxiously loud exhaust system.

I had even located two pairs of nice, used valve covers for the 348 to replace the rusted and mistreated chrome set that was on the car when Kim and I took ownership of it.

But one of the big spooky mysteries yet to be solved was the engine. It was obvious that the drooling, misfiring slug in the car was in no condition to power us reliably to Carrera glory.

Rebuilding the old engine would be costly, even if all of the parts could be reconditioned and reused when I tore the engine down. If I could get by with just the minimum amount of machine work and new parts, I figured I would still have $2,000 invested.

If there was a problem with the block, crank or a head casting, I would probably have to locate another engine.

In addition to the expense, an engine rebuild is relatively time consuming. The actual assembly is no real biggie, but carting the parts off to the machine shop, waiting for the work to get finished while the shop procrastinates, ordering the parts, carting everything back home... you get the idea, it all takes time.

I started prowling the internet for a running, complete 348 engine for less than what it would cost to rebuild mine. Within a couple of weeks I located a perfect candidate just a few hours away.

The owner said he had purchased an old Impala believing that the engine was a 409. When he found out that what he had bought was actually an Impala with the nearly identical-looking, but less-desirable 348, he tracked down a 409 for his car, and spent large sums of money having it rebuilt and installed-Now, he was just trying to recoup some of his money by selling the unwanted 348.

It certainly sounded promising. In the eBay listing for the 348 the seller boasted, often in all capital letters and with excessive amounts of punctuation: "Less than 5,000 miles on motor," and that the engine was, "Complete from manifold to oil pan, water pump to flywheel." "READY TO INSTALL!! ADJUST VALVES AND GO!!! MINT CONDITION!!"

Included in the listing were pictures of what presumably was the engine for sale, gleaming in the engine bay of a Chevrolet. It was dressed up with finned aluminum valve covers and assorted other glittering geegaws so I figured it had probably spent more time being admired at ice cream stands than racing across Mexico at 100-plus mph.

I quizzed the seller over the phone about the condition of the engine and he raved about how well it ran but said that he had always wanted a 409 Impala. His mechanic had discovered that the engine was in fact a 348 when they tried to adapt a set of high-performance 409 heads to it. This was also apparently when he discovered that the engine had "less than 5,000 miles," running time on it as the eBay listing noted.

I decided to take the risk and bid on the 348. At $1,510 I became its proud owner and headed off with my old pickup and my old dog Greta to claim my prize.

The seller showed up at the appointed meeting place and led me to the house where the engine was stored. It was indeed a 348, though between the time that he'd written the optimistic description and the time I arrived to collect the engine, some small details had, uh, mysteriously changed.

For instance one of the head bolts was missing, apparently robbed when the guy's mechanic was assembling the 409 for his Impala. The water pump was also not the one shown on the chromed-up engine pictured in the listing, but rather one of unknown origin. Also, the oil pan was dented and had been repaired at some point in its life. Though it didn't seem to be leaking, it should probably be removed and inspected, I figured.

Hmmmm ... so much for: "READY TO INSTALL!! ADJUST VALVES AND GO!!!"

I was counting on the fact that the guy wasn't a bald-faced liar and forked over the $1,510 in cash. Though I had my doubts, the engine did look otherwise clean.

Once the 348 was on my garage floor, I immediately yanked its heads off for a look into the cylinders. It was in good condition but probably had more like 35,000 miles on it than 5,000, judging from the slight carbon build-up on the tops of the pistons and the glazing evident on the cylinder walls.

That I could live with. But what gave me goosebumps was the fact that an electrode had broken off one of the spark plugs and dropped into the cylinder. There was some slight scoring evident but no serious damage to the engine or the valves. The broken piece of the electrode was still lying in the cylinder, too. I wondered if it had ever been run with the broken plug — maybe just turned over a few times?

Still, why had the electrode chipped off the spark plug in the first place? Wrong plugs? Improper piston clearance?

I emailed the seller to quiz him a little about the broken spark plug and his reasons for thinking the engine was freshly rebuilt, which it clearly wasn't.

In his response, written in all capital letters, he graciously offered to refund my money, provided I wanted to drive 2.5 hours to bring the engine back to him. He didn't, however, answer any of my questions, though he did question why I had taken the engine apart to inspect it.

Of course, if the engine hadn't been missing a head bolt, which he never mentioned until I arrived to pick it up, I probably would have taken him at his word and installed it. But the head bolts had to be loosened and properly torqued all at once. Moreover, there was no point in replacing one head gasket.

I suggested that, instead of me driving another five hours, he refund some of my money and that I keep the engine. With his caps-lock key firmly depressed the owner replied angrily, accusing me of trying to hustle him and saying that I shouldn't have expected perfection from a used engine.

O.K. Whatever. It was only $1,500 and I did have what appeared to be a sound engine. I rotated the 348 over again and again by hand on my engine stand, taking careful measurements and trying to determine why the spark plug had failed. Everything seemed O.K. so I blew out the dust and bolted it back together, fingers tightly crossed.

With the 348 sitting in the Impala's engine bay, I spent the next couple days reinstalling the fuel system, wiring, ignition and exhaust—this time more carefully than I had during the test-fit stage.

Finally, I twisted the key and the stray 348 took its first breath of LPG and roared to life. The oil pressure gauge shot up to 60 pounds immediately. Despite the minor drama, all indications were that this engine was in far better shape then the one the car came with and would probably have enough usable life to take an 1,800-mile pounding across Mexico.

The new-to-me 348 with the mysterious broken spark plug electrode sports a fresh coat of rattle-can Chevrolet Orange and looks at home in the Impala's spiffed-up engine bay. Though I had my doubts, that engine turned out to be rugged and reliable.

# Chapter 10
## No truck? No problem

**W**hile the Impala was taking shape as well as could be expected (considering a writer was doing most of the work) and I seemed to have a crew of stouthearted adventurers assembled, there was yet another fairly serious problem: We didn't have anything to actually pull the trailer I had borrowed for the trip.

My beloved Chevy truck was 35 years old at the time, 90 percent worn out and offers less-than-luxurious seating for three across its tattered bench seat. My original plan had been to bum a truck from an automaker through my connections in their media relations departments, but as you might recall, no one was willing to risk sending a new pickup to the southern tip of Mexico and, hopefully, back again.

I decided I would sell my old truck and purchase something that would make the trip reliably and comfortably hauling four people, one dilapidated race car, a small inventory of spare parts and every tool I owned including my generator, welder and torches. Ken, however, thought selling my pickup was a bad idea and suggested that we go in halves on something for the trip, take it very easy with it along the way and then immediately sell it to recoup our money once we returned.

We went to look at a used one-ton Chevrolet van with a 6.5-liter turbo diesel V-8 engine. It had been a camper conversion at one point in its life and though a little seedy inside, the owner had kept meticulous service records detailing every oil change, windshield wiper blade replacement and tire rotation the van had ever undergone in the 60,000 miles that he'd driven it. The asking price was $6,500. Not exactly a giveaway, but cheap enough, Ken and I figured, for a vehicle that had obviously not been mistreated.

We discussed the merits of this plan on the ride

home and decided we would let the owner sit on it for a little while, with hopes of buying it slightly cheaper.

I was home for about an hour when Kim called from a friend's house in Texas. He had just returned from his latest seafaring assignment and purchased a mid 1990s Chevrolet pickup truck—a one-ton, diesel dually with an extended cab. The perfect rig for dragging a car, four guys and assorted sundries to the Carrera.

The truck had lived its entire life in the dry Southwest so it was remarkably solid, but had 240,000 miles showing on its odometer and boasted a suspicious engine noise, Kim explained, over the phone. Still he couldn't pass up the $5,000 asking price.

Kim had also purchased an open car trailer and was going to use it to haul home a 1956 Ford station wagon he'd bought from a fellow merchant marine.

Kim tore into his newly acquired truck's engine in an Austin, Texas, parking lot and discovered several collapsed lifters. He replaced the faulty parts, bolted everything back together and pointed the truck for home, stopping in Alabama to pick up his old Ford.

All seemed well until about a month later, when Kim was leaving my house, the truck's engine checked out in spectacular fashion. Upon later inspection it appeared that a connecting rod broke, the piston became cocked in the bore and the renegade pieces proceeded to drive a hole in the engine's cylinder wall. White smoke bellowed out of the truck's exhaust as the water from the coolant system flooded the cylinders and the whole shebang sputtered to a halt on the side of the road.

Kim hiked back to my house and called a tow truck to haul the pickup to Ken's garage. If that truck thought it was getting off easy, it was sorely mistaken.

In about a week, Kim had the truck running again — but not before buying a new engine, turbo, injectors and a warehouse full of small, miscellaneous parts.

It was a superhuman effort, both physically and financially, but at least armed with a spanking-new engine we figured this mighty truck would complete the journey worry-free.

# Chapter 11
## We're going to make it... right?

As the weeks evaporated, I grew ever more panicked and spent more and more hours under, inside and around the Impala. Kim tore into the spooky taillight wiring and stayed on the job until the directionals, brake lights and taillights were functioning properly. My father had offered to weld in the roll cage, so I gladly took him up on it.

Kim mounted the LPG tank permanently in the trunk and made the sheetmetal firewall between the trunk and the passenger compartment, where the back seat would normally go. We purchased a set of front seats out of a demolished Dodge Neon at a

Kim (above) fabricates a sheetmetal firewall between the Impala's trunk and the interior. My Dad (below) welds up one of the floor plates used to anchor the roll cage.

junkyard and I made brackets to mount them in the Impala in place of the original bench.

Slowly we checked stuff off the list of the Impala's maladies that I had nailed to the garage wall. Still, there were a 1,000 details that we weren't quite as successful with.

For instance, we wouldn't be running a rally clock like serious competitors but we at least needed a functioning, resettable mechanical odometer in the car.

So I bought an Autometer speedo then tracked down a cable and a plastic drive gear, all of which were missing when we bought the Impala. I made a bracket to hang the speedometer, routed the cable and installed the drive gear one Sunday. A trip down the driveway revealed that all of my efforts had been a huge waste of time. The needle was pegged at 0 mph and all I could figure was that the gear inside the transmission was probably faulty because the speedo worked when I spun it over with an electric drill. This was typical of the way work on the car (or any old car) often progressed. I would dive into a task that seemed like it would be simple enough for a monkey to complete and four hours later I would still be toiling away, greasy, frustrated, drenched with sweat and cursing wildly.

At times like that, my sanity tends to peel away like cheap paint revealing the ugly, angry, paranoid defeatist that's always inside me. On this particular wasted day, I had become so disgusted with the whole project that I actually called Gerie Bledsoe and asked him what the chances of getting a refund on our $4,500 Carrera entry fee would be, just a couple of weeks before the race was to kick off.

"Uh, probably not too good, Mike. Why? What's wrong?"

Ten seconds into the conversation I had calmed down and felt silly for wanting to throw in the towel over a busted speedometer, but I explained the situation to Gerie nonetheless.

He listened to my whining and then talked me away from the edge of the precipice.

"Look Mike, honestly, you don't even really need a speedometer or an odometer for that matter. You can get by with just a digital wrist watch. Stop sweating the little details and make sure you've got the major stuff covered. If the car runs, stops and has all of the essential safety equipment in it you'll be fine."

I hung up the phone feeling slightly less defeated, a

little stupid for calling Gerie to whine and still pretty unsure of this whole endeavor. With just about a month to go, it seemed like there was too much to do, too much money to spend and too many unanswered questions.

Miraculously the day before we were to leave for the race, most of the necessary work had been done and I drove the Impala to work just to spend a little more time behind the wheel. Kim and I had only taken it on one hour-long shakedown cruise during which I piloted the Impala while he followed with his truck and trailer in case the car broke. The Impala ran great and it looked, well, O.K.... from 20 or maybe 50 feet away. It was kind of a sore spot with me, but I hadn't had the time or the resources to address either the car's so-so red paint or its blistering body work — which seemed to have deteriorated even more from the night the Impala arrived at my house until the day we left for Mexico. There was also a patina of rust over a lot of the chrome plated trim parts, not unlike the junkyard bicycle I rode as a kid.

The night before our departure, I was supposed to take the car to Scott's garage for a front-end alignment. By the time I arrived back home from work it was pouring rain and, according to the gauge on the fuel tank, I was low on fuel. (One of the problems with an LPG fuel system is range anxiety as there aren't filling stations on every street corner.)

I called Ken and arranged a tow in case the car ran out of fuel en route to Scott's and headed out into the night.

The Impala made the trip on whatever was left in the tank and Scott had the car handling like new by the time I left his shop. That night, when I wheeled back in my driveway, it started to feel like, despite the Impala's high front end, blistering paint and lack of a functioning speedometer in a time-distance rally, we might actually be competing in this race after all.

# Chapter 12
## Ready or not! (Not)

Suddenly it was October 16, the day we select-
ed to ease out of town, leaving home and
family behind to seek government-sanctioned
speed and glory in Mexico.

Kim and I had badly blown the noon departure
time we'd set for ourselves, leaving Ken and Scott
to hang around Ken's repair shop — the appointed
meeting place — while we screwed around with
stuff that probably should've been attended to weeks
before.

At Ken's garage, we topped off the Impala's fuel
tank with propane and, for good measure, tossed a

few more random supplies into the trailer that Ken and Scott thought to bring. This included Scott's winch: "In case we have to pull you guys out of a ravine!" he cheerfully explained. Then we finally hit the road — four hours and 11 minutes later than planned.

About 100 miles from home, just shy of the New York State line and 3,500 shy of our destination, Kim reported that the clutch pedal had suddenly gone limp under his boot.

The problem turned out to be mysterious pinholes in the line that supplies fluid to the clutch's hydraulic slave cylinder. So, on a stretch of sharply descending Route 84, somewhere near the Pennsylvania border, Ken and Kim performed a makeshift repair on the line and Scott assumed the role of pedal man, pumping the clutch until he felt some pressure building in the line.

It wasn't long before the clutch was working and, over a round of fresh hand cleaner and paper towels, we were congratulating ourselves for having the ingenuity and skill to pull the old truck together and keep the trip rolling.

The repair lasted approximately 500 feet before the

Some periodic roadside repair was necessary to keep the truck rolling. Luckily we had a lot of tools and a lot of professional mechanics. That's your author at far left offering worthless suggestions while Kim and Ken do all of the actual work.

—PHOTO BY SCOTT BENWAY

line ruptured again.

We cruised along in high gear discussing our options and decided we should find a Home Depot where we could purchase some compression fittings that would hold the line together. Near Hazelton, Pennsylvania, we limped off Route 84, made it to the Home Depot parking lot and set up shop. Inside the store we rummaged for supplies. Kim bought an array of tubing connectors and splices while I opted for a family pack of paper towels, more hand cleaner and a new flashlight — figuring all of the above would come in very handy. I headed for the bathroom to wash up and called my wife to tell her about our already misdirected trip.

I won't kid you, dear reader. By the time we left for Mexico, the realities of spending money that I didn't really have to build a race car that I didn't really know how to build, had become like a yearlong hangover following that night I got drunk reading a car magazine and talked Kim into entering La Carrera Panamericana. So hearing Kathy's voice on the phone made me want to turn around and head for home.

Meanwhile, back out in the parking lot, attacking problems as fast as they dared to pop up and challenge him, Ken had fashioned a new splice for the ailing clutch line. It was a fairly well-engineered fix, but lasted only a few miles before it broke again.

We crawled on into the night, figuring we'd stop to repair the line again only when we had run out of fuel.

In less than 24 hours we repaired the line five times. The final fix was after a short roadside sleep break and breakfast at a truck stop in Virginia.

With the clutch line apparently conquered, we hit the highway, hammering south through Virginia. After five blissful hours of trouble-free motoring, Kim announced the truck had lost its lost power steering, and the temperature was starting to climb. We figured the serpentine belt was the culprit. In a gas station parking lot near a sign happily welcoming our forlorn troop to scenic Salem, Virginia, we discovered that not only was the serpentine belt off, but the water pump pulley had broken in three places and was wobbling uselessly on the end of the shaft.

We eyed a dirt pull-off on a short side street near the gas station and decided it was the perfect spot to try and reconstruct the pulley. Kim grabbed a piece of steel we'd brought along and using part of the pulley as a template, we drew the outline of a circle on the steel and cut it out with the torch. Scott trimmed up the new patch with the torch and grinder while I hooked up the generator and welder and prepared to weld it to the ailing pulley. Ken and Kim meanwhile were making some shims out of a piece of flatstock trying to level up all of the engine accessories to account for the slightly thicker, rebuilt pulley.

In about two hours, the pulley in place, we were

I probably would've voted to just leave everything on the side of the road and walk home at this point, but Kim wasn't letting me quit. Here, I'm welding a new center into the broken water pump pulley, fashioned from a piece of steel we'd brought along.

fueled up and on the road again. That night, only the second night of our trip, we treated ourselves to a room at a Best Western near Knoxville, Tennessee.

The following morning at a diner next door to the hotel, we decided we needed to locate a Chevrolet dealer where we could pick up a new pulley and clutch line to have as spares. A dealer near Memphis had both parts on the shelf.

After the side trip to Memphis, we made a beeline straight through the South and Texas stopping only for fuel and food.

By 11 a.m. the next day, we were in Laredo, Texas — our last stop in the U.S. We dined like true world travelers at an International House of Pancakes and hit a big box department store to buy a stereo for the truck as the original had quit on the way. The weather was what you would expect from South Texas — hot and dry as the inside of a kiln. Ken was determined to get the air conditioning in the truck working, so we wandered around Laredo in search of an auto parts store where Kim bought an A/C charging kit.

Around noon, we breezed through a border checkpoint in Nuevo Laredo, Mexico, where the border officers recognized us as La Carrera Panamericana hopefuls. One of them directed us to a vehicle permit station where we wrestled with a pile of Mexican government motor vehicle forms.

A minor snag in the title of our borrowed trailer—caught by a sharp-eyed official—resulted in a brief negotiation with the authorities, but we cleared the whole thing up in short order.

Out in the parking lot, a few pesos lighter and

armed with some official-looking stickers for the windshields of Kim's truck and the Impala, we took our last homesick looks across the Rio Grande at the giant flag waving over U.S. soil.

The trip to Mexico had been fraught with sleeplessness, mechanical failure and some bad route selection, but the guys hadn't thrown me out of the moving truck and headed back for home, so I was calling the trip an unqualified success so far.

# Chapter 13
## It sure looked a lot shorter on the map

Our plan had been to shove off at noon on a Saturday, then hook up with Jose Rubio and his team (whom we had met through my discussions with Gerie Bledsoe) in Pachuca, Mexico, on Tuesday. We would then just tag along and let his Carrera-seasoned gang lead us to the starting line. Meeting with Team Rubio was also important because Jose, who owned and drove the only other LPG-fueled car in the race, was a propane dealer and had graciously offered to let us fuel up out of the back of his delivery truck, which he was bringing along to ensure a constant supply of gas.

Unfortunately, just outside Nashville, Tennessee, I had to ask Kathy to phone ahead and tell Jose we were running too far behind to make the rendezvous. This sucked because it meant we would have to navigate to the start of the race in Tuxtla on our own.

In theory this should be easy, particularly one would think, for guys about to compete in a long-distance road rally. It should've gone something like this:

1. Open map (this was before smart phones and my GPS at the time was useless in parts of Mexico);
2. Pick the straightest red or blue line on a major highway heading south (Hey how about the Panamerican Highway route?);
3. Drive.

Our biggest mistake was trying too hard to avoid traveling anywhere near Mexico City. So, in order to circumvent what might of amounted to a couple hours of hassle, we lumbered along the Gulf Coast of Mexico on rough, narrow, rural roads easily turning about 20 hours of driving into a three-day excursion and burning up a lot of fuel, time and patience in the process.

What the maps don't tell you is that many of the secondary roads in Mexico are paved by fourth-string asphalt crews. We actually saw one road being black-topped in the middle of the night by the glow of a few pairs of pickup truck headlights.

Mistake number two was not exchanging our American dollars for a sack full of pesos at the border. While American dollars are more widely accepted in Mexico than pesos are in the U.S., there are still a lot of places that won't take gringo money. Like for instance, Pemex stations—the state-owned gas/diesel stations — and toll booths, of which there are plenty.

Don't expect to live off your "universally accepted" credit cards in Mexico either. A lot of places around that country don't want your plastic.

So that gives you a good sense of the spirit of our maiden voyage through Mexico — lost, aggravated, most of the time without cash and worrying that the truck was going to strand us.

Before pulling out of the gritty border town of Nuevo Laredo we stopped for fuel at a Pemex. The attendant willingly took our American money, so we paid the man and headed south on what my road atlas said was Route 2 — a narrow, desolate path through the center of nothing and nowhere, flanked by barren plains of brown scrub brush.

We pressed on, reaching the sketchy border town of Reynosa by sunset. We hadn't stopped for sleep since Knoxville, Tennessee, which seemed fine with Kim, but was clearly wearing on Scott, Ken and me. Kim is an iron man who can function without rest for days. In fact, he actually seems to enjoy torturing himself with sleep deprivation, the way other people might find comfort in classical music or a deep tissue massage.

During one of our many long overnight conversations on the road, Kim told me that while serving on the U.S.S Aspro, a now-decomissioned Sturgeon-class, nuclear, fast-attack Navy submarine, it was common practice for the crew to work days on end without sleep, apparently in preparation for some protracted battle beneath the waves of the Pacific where they were deployed. A comforting thought—a 300-foot-long, submarine crewed by a bunch of sleep-starved kids armed to the teeth with weapons designed to sink bigger Soviet subs. It's amazing that the world didn't vaporize under a half-dozen mushroom clouds before Reagan was able to deficit-spend the USSR into bankruptcy.

During the trip, Ken had taken to calling Kim "The

Wheel Nazi," because Kim only grudgingly let anyone else take the steering wheel for fear that we would slow down or pull over altogether.

While we napped, Kim kept his boot planted against the floor boards growing increasingly more serious and more determined. Picture Captain Ahab in a baseball cap and T-shirt with a death grip on the controls of a Chevy pickup and you'll get the idea.

The problem was, the crappy roads we chose were against us the entire way. Chasms in the pavement shook the front end of the truck near to breaking it seemed, while the trailer, full of our worldly possessions and the Impala, bobbed along behind us.

Day ran endlessly into night and night into day as we slithered and shook along coastal highways and byways, passing through a string of brightly painted Mexican communities. We were awed by breathtaking views of the Gulf of Mexico lapping up against broad sandy beaches dotted by quaint little Mexican resorts. If this were a Rick Steves travel guide book, you'd be reading about the many wonderful places along Mexico's Gulf Shore, where you could plan your next romantic getaway. But the only thing romantic about the getaway we were on was the

Kim's truck pictured somewhere in Mexico. I have no idea where, so please don't ask.

notion that we might actually find the race before all of the other cars had crossed the finish line. In the best case scenario, the race would pass us going the other way so we could just turn around and follow them all back to the U.S.

Often we found that the route numbers listed on our map didn't correspond with the actual roads on which we were traveling and my GPS could only tell us the direction we were heading.

About five hours outside Veracruz, the beautiful coastal resort city, we came to an on-ramp for a toll road blocked by rubble, rocks and severed tree limbs.

A short distance ahead, we came across a couple of shirtless kids standing out in the road holding flags that appeared to have been made from their shirts.

"Veracruz?" Kim said to them.

"Si," they replied, pointing to another ramp for the same highway which wasn't blocked with rubble and debris. We pulled a U-turn and headed for the ramp.

At the side of the road, a disheveled old man was sitting in a makeshift shack with a rope stretched across the entrance to the highway ahead. He approached the truck and Kim waved him off with a $5 bill.

"Gracias," he said, smiling and waving. He then shuffled over and dropped the flimsy rope letting us pass.

So basically this old guy and these kids had blocked the only way to the highway, set up a makeshift private, for-profit, toll booth and managed to swindle $5 out of us. A few miles up the road, we came across yet another group of guys with another rope stretched across the road, collecting tolls. Since we figured we'd already paid our way, Kim mashed his boot to the floor and, at the sight of that big grill guard bearing down on them at 80 mph, the ragtag highway robbers dropped the rope and scattered.

We continued to meander through Mexico, lost, tired, and forking over money at mostly legitimate toll booths, draining whatever pesos we could trade our American dollars for at Pemex stations.

Roads frequently led us not to places promised on the map, but to confusing, ill-marked intersections where it was often impossible to guess which way to go.

We asked directions at every fill-up and, along the way, from taxi and delivery truck drivers. In one small town we wandered into, we spotted a friendly looking older guy in a Corona beer truck parked alongside the road. Kim hopped up on the running board of the truck, map in hand, and proceeded to point where we needed to go.

The driver nodded and smiled, thought for a moment how best to bridge the language barrier then began to gesture in a forward, chopping motion with his left forearm.

"Pista, pista!" he said.

Kim looked at him befuddled then squinted down the road in the direction he was pointing — perhaps hoping that he would suddenly spot some clue that we hadn't noticed while staring down the same stretch of highway for 10 to15 minutes.

Realizing he wasn't getting through to Kim, the truck driver grabbed the map and pointed emphatically to one of the many random crisscrossing blue and red lines that allegedly represented real roads.

"Pista! Pista!" he said. "Pista! Pista!"

"This road?" Kim replied, joining the driver in pointing at the map. "We need to take this road to Tuxtla?"

"Si!" he said, poking his index finger at the useless piece of paper one more time for good measure and then resuming the forceful chopping motion with his left arm. "Pista! Piiiiiiistaa!

Kim hopped off the running board of the truck, nodding his head and thanking the driver profusely. "Gracias!"

"Do you know what he was talking about?" I asked Kim as we walked back down the road toward our truck.

"I don't have a clue," Kim said.

We climbed back in the cab where Ken was waiting in the back seat. "What did he say?" Ken asked, hopeful that we might finally make some headway.

I imitated the truck driver's wild gestures with my left arm and said, "Pista! Pista!"

"What's that mean?" Ken asked.

"I have no idea," I said. "You're now as completely confused as we are."

# Chapter 14
## See, I told you we'd make it

Onward we wandered, until somehow we managed to stumble up to the hotel that the Carrera's organizers were using as the events' home base. It was Thursday night—we were more than 24 hours late, but it was a miracle that we were there at all.

The chief safety inspector looked over our car by flashlight out on the unlit access road to the hotel. He wasn't entirely impressed by everything he saw, but took pity on us and passed us anyway. "Look. Guys. Please," he said. "Just take it easy out there. We don't want anyone getting hurt."

We woke up on race day rested, refreshed and completely clueless about where we were supposed to start the race or how exactly to get there.

Kim hadn't been able to locate the route books the previous night because we arrived at the hotel so late. We had managed to get the La Carrera Panamerica door decals with our car number on them but according to the rules, there were a number of sponsor decals that were supposed to be displayed on the car, as well as the names and blood types of the piloto and co-piloto.

We also had no way of knowing if the Impala had enough fuel range to even make it to the first fuel stop, nor did we know if Jose Rubio's propane truck would be waiting for us.

We unloaded the Impala on a short dirt road near the hotel and tried to figure out exactly what needed to be done. It was a beautiful morning: Probably cool for southern Mexico and overcast. The smell of gasoline fumes hung in the air and the crackle of race engines rang out as drivers hustled off to the starting arch.

I was already sacked from the previous week of hardcore travel, sleeping only a few hours every night on the backseat of the truck. How Kim was even standing, I had no idea. I was worried about getting lost or running out of fuel, or both so I suggested that we skip that day's racing.

"Let's drive on to the next town, Oaxaca, where we can regroup, get the car ready, get our route books and attack this thing right the following day," I said.

Without those route books—there was supposed to be one for the crews driving the support trucks and one for the racers—I feared Scott and Ken, driving the truck, would get separated from Kim and I driving the Impala. Or one of us would get lost in the mountains of Chiapas.

Kim was hearing nothing of quitting this race that had been my stupid idea to enter in the beginning. He marched back toward the hotel, apparently in search of a route book.

I drove the Impala back on the trailer and headed off to find him.

On the way, I ran into Gerie Bledsoe who was hurrying to get his race car to the starting line.

Never having met Gerie in person, but recognizing his race car from photos, I walked over to introduce myself.

"Hey, glad to see you made it," Gerie said. "I heard you had some trouble with your truck."

"Yeah, we got in late last night and we're not really ready. I think we're going to skip today and head up to Oaxaca. Then start fresh tomorrow."

"Oh really? Why? If I were you, I'd just drive down and start anyway. At least get some points for showing up." Hmmm. Maybe Kim was right to be a little tired of my worrying.

"Thanks, Gerie, I'll catch up with you later."

I ran back to the trailer where Scott and Ken were milling around.

"Let's unload it," I said to Scott. "Kim's right we need to have a go at this thing."

With a click of the key, the Impala roared to life and backed off the trailer. Ken and Scott immediately jumped on it and began tying up loose ends. Kim showed up with a few pages he had photocopied from another team's book.

I unpackaged my brand-spanking-new firesuit and slipped it on. We jumped in the car and Ken fidgeted with my safety harness.

"You guys have to get hooked up with another crew and follow them!" I yelled to Ken over the roar of the Impala's wide-open exhaust.

Ken replied with one of his reassuring smiles and a nod. "We'll be fine. We'll follow somebody. Just go!"

Kim was in the passenger seat suited up, so I stuffed the Impala in gear and roared past our trailer. The crappy old car, with its half-assed steering and antiquated brakes felt good to me. I "blipped" the throttle, just like the guys I'd read about in magazines, when I was a kid and grabbed second gear, then third as we hauled down the road away from the hotel.

Just like that, we were in the Carrera.

We were racers!

In less than a mile, it became very evident that we weren't quite in the Carrera yet because we were lost. Again. This time in downtown Tuxtla.

A cop directing traffic at an intersection pointed the general direction to us while Kim tried to figure out where the hell we were going with his photo-copied route map. Tuxtla is a fair-sized city and the morning commute was in full swing. Plus, the streets were lined with cars and people all out to see the start of the race.

Kim was still a little green to the rally navigating business, but he would learn very quickly—like he

learned high-school chemistry during the last month
of the school year and left me to go to summer
school.

At the start of the race we drove past the rows
of meticulously prepared and neatly painted vintage machinery in our rough and rusted, unmuffled
jalopy/junker.

Man, the cars in this race all looked *soooo* nice.
Corvettes, Porsches, Mustangs, a sea of Studebakers.
Most of them sporting big tires, disc brakes, and
stout racing stances, where the front end is hunkered
down and actually level with the back end. We took
our place, nose-high and dead last in the 70-car field
because we hadn't made it to the qualifying event the
previous day.

I rolled to a stop at the rear of the lineup behind
a bright-red '65 Chevelle that I figured was racing in
our class, "Historic C." There was also a Plymouth
Barracuda that had actually made the drive from the
U.S. border to the start of the race.

Kim was amped up, despite having slept a total of
about three minutes in the last week and he immediately jumped out of the car.

"I'm going to see if I can get some time sheets," he

said, referring to a form that race officials, along the race route, mark at various checkpoints so that racers have a record of their time.

I climbed out and struck up a conversation with the driver of the Barracuda. I can't remember much of the conversation but one statement he made sticks in my mind.

"At least where I'm from, in California we don't have to deal with rust," he said, laughing a little and nodding toward a hole in the Impala's quarter panel that had opened up when my father and I were installing the roll cage. The more my old man beat on the steel floor plates he welded in to anchor the bottom of the cage, the more the rust chips and body filler dropped from the Impala's badly preserved body cavities. Looking at all of the gleaming machinery parked on the starting grid, I was even more sensitive about the fact that I hadn't gotten around to doing any paint and body work on the car.

Soon enough, it was time to take the green flag. One by one, the race cars rolled up the ramp to the starting arch, the drivers said a few pithy words to a guy holding a microphone and then roared down the ramp that led to a spectator-lined street.

That's us rolling up to the starting line dead last as onlookers admired the Impala's blistered paint and body work.

—PHOTO BY SCOTT BENWAY

Among our numerous pre-race worries was that we would run out of propane along the way, since we hadn't had time to meet up with Jose Rubio before the event. As we were waiting in line, Jose's sister ran up to the side of the car, introduced herself and told us that she was glad to see we had made it. Jose, she said, had sent the propane truck up to the first fuel stop the night before, so as long as we made it that far, we were golden.

The Impala may have looked like the product of a high-school auto body class project, circa 1985, but its used, cleaned-up and regasketed 348 engine, with the mysterious broken spark plug, felt like it could pull a bus load of tourists and their fanny packs up the side of an Aztec pyramid. The engine sounded nasty too — the open exhaust system I'd put on the car cackled demonically at the slightest hit of the throttle. Scott's alignment job had made the car 95 percent less frightening, and the brake adjustment that Kim had given it a few nights before we left had actually made it possible to stop the Impala with normal pressure applied with one foot.

The Impala was the last car up the starting ramps, but there was still a crowd of spectators lined up shoulder-to-shoulder on both sides of the street as far as the eye could see down Tuxtla's main drag. I whacked the throttle hard a few times in low gear as I approached the ramp, the Impala snarled and lurched forward like an animal. Kim smiled and nodded affirmatively as the crowd cheered.

"Are you ready to race?" The announcer shouted to us. "Not exactly, but this is probably as good as it gets," I yelled back. When the flagman waved us off I decided it was my duty to make the last car off the line the loudest. I wound up every gear long and slow, letting the RPMs build to a deafening crescendo.

Then, when I shifted, I double-clutched each gear, snapping the throttle in between stabs of the clutch pedal.

Guys on the side of the road were pumping their arms and howling as the Impala thundered past. I blew the horn a few times and they cheered louder. The scene was totally, unbelievably, goose-bump-raising cool.

Unfortunately, the same could not be said of the Impala's engine. In no more than a half mile of driving, the temperature gauge needle had climbed to 190 degrees and was rising. Back home, in the balmy, sea-level Northeast air, the car refused to budge past 180 and on cool days it regularly ran 160. Mexico's soaring altitudes and soaring temperatures were a whole different deal. Suddenly I was regretting my decision not to upgrade to a four-core radiator.

Nearing the end of the crowded street, I let the RPMs drop and immediately stirred the shifter into the high-gear slot in hopes of giving the engine a break. We took a right turn onto a nice, winding, two-lane road and cruised briefly in high gear until we caught up to the tail end of the Carrera field. In the race's first few miles, there were already cars pulled off to the side with mechanical problems — cars that all looked considerably better than the Impala.

The temperature gauge had settled on 190 degrees, which certainly wasn't a problem. If it ran there all day, we would be in good shape. It was only about 8:30 a.m. though, and I knew the hottest part of the day and the toughest speed stages lay ahead.

# Chapter 15

## You can't get away with that kind of stuff nowadays

The first speed stage was just a few miles from Tuxtla near a place called Ocozocoautla (pronounced "Ocozocoautla"). Kim and I donned our new helmets and buckled our five-point safety restraints for the first time. We inched forward in line as car after car roared off to try and tame the diabolically twisting mountain road.

In case you skimmed by the explanation earlier, during the Carrera's speed stages, the road is closed off to traffic for a few miles, allowing drivers to run wide open and use up as much of the blacktop as necessary. The dozen or so short speed stages run each day are linked by longer transit stages, which involve navigating over public roads in traffic while trying to maintain a speed average.

Our first speed run was smooth and as fast as can be expected from a stock, rust-blistered 1961 Impala shod with cheapo white walls and carrying its front end two inches higher than the rear. It was also stupid, crazy fun for a couple of guys from Upstate New York.

The early stages of the Carrera are run through the towering mountain peaks in southern Mexico. The two-lane road we were racing on appeared to have been chiseled and blasted into the mountains following whatever route its builders could manage to cut through. The asphalt was in excellent condition by New York standards, but the corners were sharp enough to cut glass. Virtually all of the roads that the race organizers chose for speed sections in the early parts of the Carrera can be summed up like this: On one side there's a massive, jagged rock wall eager for the chance to grind and pulverize your car like a giant fist. On the other side, a cliff that you could parachute off.

My cornering technique on these roads had less
to do with finding apexes than finding a way to keep
a 4,000-pound sedan and its two passengers from
plunging to their deaths.

I snuggled the Impala's front fenders up against
the rock walls in every turn and let the back end hang
out, figuring that the driver and passenger seats would
wind up going where the front wheels were pointed.
So, as long as they weren't pointed toward a cliff, we'd
be OK. If we crashed into the side of a mountain,
the rocks would have to go through that grossly over-
weight engine to chew on us. For me this wasn't a race
to win, but rather a race to survive so that Kim and I
could tell our loved ones about it as soon as possible.

Driving the Impala on a straight highway at 55 mph
was a challenge. But careening up and down twisting
mountain roads, sawing at that giant red and white
steering wheel and pumping the fading drum brakes
— all while trying to maintain the appearance of
being in a race — required constant and serious attention. Before I drifted the Impala into a turn, I would
have to take up the slack in the steering box with the
wheel — which amounted to between a quarter and a
half a turn. It wasn't a big deal on corners, at the end

of a straightaway, but switchbacks that required turning right and then left or left and then right were a serious bitch.

It was also immediately apparent that the stock brakes — as Kim had predicted — were woefully inadequate. For commuter car use they were fine. But with me furiously grinding the shoes into the drums mile after mile, trying to buy myself enough time to set up the loose steering for the next turn, they overheated and withered like banana peels in the Mexican sun.

Kim meanwhile was screaming out directions from our makeshift, photocopied route book, trying to be heard through the helmets and over the roaring 348.

With some semblance of racing, we made it through the first section unscathed. As we blasted past the pair of cones and a flag-waving race official marking the end of the stage, the Impala's temperature gauge was pegged on 230 degrees.

We pulled up alongside another group of clipboard wielding officials and received our time for the section, which Kim recorded on our time card. The Impala's temperature was stable. It wasn't rising, but it wasn't dropping either.

I was eager to get rolling down the highway and get some air circulating around that massive chunk of cast iron under the Impala's hood.

As we clicked off the miles, the temperature dropped and I relaxed a little. Rolling through Mexican villages along the way meant slowing down for what the Mexicans call topes which amount to speed bumps built smack dab in the middle of the public road. I enjoyed the topes during the race because they were a favorite gathering place for race fans and kids who would wait there for the cars to slow down enough for a close-up glimpse and cheer as we passed. Most of the topes were well marked, but occasionally they weren't. Hit one of them at speed and you could count on doing untold damage to your car's underpinnings.

At the midway point of the first day, we rolled into the rest area on time, with fuel to spare, and finally met Jose Rubio face to face. He turned out to be a solidly built man with the hands of a guy who has worked for a living his whole life and an impish grin that tells you he's learned a few things along the way.

In Mexico, he operated an LPG gas business and performed LPG vehicle conversions.

Jose's co-driver Hugo Zenil was a bear of a man, with a kind, warm smile and a quick wit. His English, too, was perfect, though he had only spent a limited amount of time in the U.S. This made me feel even more stupid for flunking foreign-language classes as well as math and science in high school.

After eyeing up Rubio's well-prepared LPG-fired Studebaker that he raced in the Turismo de Producción division, we headed to a nearby LPG station to fuel up, as Jose had already sent his truck to the next stop. The guy at the LPG filling station seemed delighted to top off the Impala's tank and spoke to us in broken English that was considerably better than our Spanish.

Other than the overheating, our first few hours in the world's greatest vintage car race were as amazing as I'd imagined.

# Chapter 16

## Hey guys, that was cool!
## Guys? Guys?

A t the end of the first day, we rolled into Oaxaca in the early evening, probably around 5 p.m., and just in time for rush-hour traffic. I had run the car past 260 degrees on the last speed stage of the day and boiled off some of the water in the radiator. Everything was fine so long as we were rolling. But in downtown Oaxaca's bumper-to-bumper rush-hour traffic, the Impala was overheating. To make matters worse, we were stumbling around lost, as usual, trying to find the finish line.

At a red light, a Toyota with a bunch of young locals pulled alongside us.

"Hey," one of them yelled (in perfect English). "Why didn't you fix the rust holes?" He motioned to the Impala's rusted rocker panel and quarter panel as the rest of them laughed.

Beaten and broke, Kim and I just frowned at each other and shook our heads in disgust.

Kim, the Impala and I would probably still be lost somewhere in Oaxaca getting laughed at by other motorists if it weren't for Team Rubio. Jose's sister and brother-in-law spotted us in traffic, pulled past us in their pickup and motioned for us to follow them. They took us through a maze of narrow side streets until we arrived at the city's beautiful old-world center square. A police officer lifted the barricades and allowed us to enter the courtyard where all of the other race cars were already parked beneath a canopy of trees and greenery. We hadn't found the official finish arch, therefore we never received points for finishing that day's racing. The Impala's temperature needle was pegged, and I was fearing for the head gaskets. But worst of all, we hadn't seen Ken and Scott since we told them to find someone to follow and left the starting line that morning. Were they OK? Lost? Had they made the trip without having to stop and remanufacture some weak part of the truck on the side of the road?

"They're probably back at the hotel already," Kim said. "I'll bet Scott hired a taxi and they followed it to the hotel once they got in town." (Kim had used that trick on the trip down to get us back on track.)

We drank beer with Team Rubio for about 45 minutes until they decided to head back to the hotel. Luckily we were staying at the same place, so Kim and I could follow them through the busy streets of Oaxaca. When I lit the engine up again, its temperature had barely dropped. It needed water badly, but I hadn't thought to install a radiator cap with a pressure relief lever, and I was afraid to try and remove the cap. We started the trek to the hotel, the temperature gauge pegged at 260.

Snaking through Oaxaca's narrow, crowded side streets, glued to the back bumper of Rubio's Studebaker, only a trickle of air was circulating through the engine compartment and the needle continued to climb.

At every opportunity, I killed the engine and coasted, hoping to save the head gaskets from popping and severely diminishing our chances of finishing this six-day gauntlet. Revving the engine in an effort to get the fan spinning only seemed to piss off the temperature gauge even more. Kim and I coasted into the Fiesta Inn and immediately began looking for a place to park the Impala so we could raise the hood to let the engine cool.

I jumped out of the car and started looking for Kim's truck and the trailer in the parking lot. Meanwhile, Kim ran up to the front desk to see if Ken and Scott had checked in.

On my way around the parking lot, I ran into Jose who told me if I wanted to fill up the Impala's propane tank, I would have to drive the car over to his delivery truck, as the driver was going to be leaving for the following day's fuel stop that night. With race cars and trailers swamping the Fiesta Inn parking lot, I knew getting just the short distance to his delivery truck was going to require a considerable amount of idling. Given the congestion, there was no way the truck was going to be able to reach the Impala where it sat.

Fearing that the short hop would cause the 348 to melt down, I grabbed a rag, gritted my teeth and slowly turned the radiator cap, hoping to get some water into the engine. As soon as the ears in the cap cleared the notches in the top of the radiator, the cap blasted off atop a geyser of scalding hot steam and filthy water. The metal cap rapped against the hood with a loud clap and ricocheted to the ground, while a dense cloud of steam smelling like wet dirt and rust filled the air in a 20-foot radius of the car.

Unfortunately, the spot I had picked to perform this impromptu radiator service was in front of the hotel lobby. Bellhops were gathering luggage on carts and hotel patrons were milling in and out of the building. No one was hurt and none of my skin was permanently damaged—which is more than I can say for the T-shirt I was wearing at the time.

Feeling like a complete idiot, as the fog of filth cleared, I immediately began apologizing profusely and asking if anyone was injured. With everyone reporting no damage, I grabbed a couple empty water bottles from inside the car and began making hurried trips to the men's room for cold water, so that I could refire the Impala and drive it over for refueling. Realizing what I was doing, one of the bellhops directed me to an outside water spigot.

With the radiator full of water again, the Impala

immediately settled down to a cool 180 degrees and I made the short trip over to Jose's truck, where his crew topped off the Impala's tank with LPG. I then swung the car around the back of the building into a fenced-in area designated for the race cars. Kim, looking very concerned, headed me off on my way back to the lobby.

"Ken and Scott haven't checked in but they left a note this afternoon saying they were on their way," he said. "They had trouble with the truck."

"Oh shit," I said. "It's 8 p.m. now. They ought to be here."

"I know, but Ken's note said he figured he was still five hours away, so maybe it's just taking them longer..."

In the hotel room, I called Ken's cell phone. No answer. Kim and I waited for the phone in our room to ring. When it finally did, it was my wife, Kathy, at about 11 p.m.

"Did Ken show up there yet?" she asked.

"No, we haven't heard anything."

"Billie Jo (Ken's wife) has called a couple of times, to find out if I've heard from you," Kathy said. "She talked to them earlier and they were having trouble with the truck."

"Alright, I'll call you when I know something," I told her.

I dropped the phone and glanced out the window of our room into the dark, unfamiliar city.

"I guess I could take the Impala and go out looking for them. If I went out that main drag we came in on..."

"Mike, that's stupid," Kim said. "You could pass them out there and not even know it. Besides, what if they're driving in on another road? No way. You don't need to get lost, too. They'll fix that truck and get it back here. Ken will not let it strand him out there."

Kim was definitely right. Wandering through southern Mexico looking for the truck in the dark was a bad idea and the odds were pretty good that if any two people in North, South or Central America could beat that truck into submission, it was Ken and Scott.

Spent from the past week's insane events, Kim caught some sleep. Meanwhile I lay awake on my bed and worried by the glare of the hotel lamp. Every hour I called Ken's phone, getting his voicemail every time.

At 3 a.m. Kathy called again.

"Billie Jo just called and said she hasn't heard from them.  Are they there?"

"Not yet. I've been calling Ken's phone every hour, but he doesn't answer. As soon as it's light out, I'm going out looking for them."

I stayed awake until 5:30 a.m. Daylight was just breaking over the city and I could make out the surrounding buildings and streets through the morning mist. Kim awoke with a start as if from a nightmare.

"Are they here?"

"No," I said. "I figured I'd head out looking for them with the Impala. You stay by the phone here and I'll call in every hour or half hour."

"Yeah, that's a good idea," Kim said "I'm going out to the parking lot, just to make sure the truck isn't out there," he said.

I pulled on my firesuit and tied the top of it down around my waist, revealing the filthy T-shirt with rust-colored stains from my previous night's bout with the Impala's radiator. That was all I had for clothes because my suitcase was in the trailer, attached to Kim's truck.

Just as I was ready to head out the door, Kim walked in.

"Look who I found out in the parking lot."

Sure enough, it was Ken and Scott, looking tired but none the worse for having completed yet another series of roadside repairs on Kim's truck somewhere in the mountains of Chiapas, and driving most of the night to Oaxaca.

The truck's hydraulic supply line to the clutch had failed several times during the previous day, just as it had on the trip down to Mexico from New York. They figured out that an exhaust leak was melting the plastic line so, out of desperation, they fashioned a new hydraulic line with a piece of steel brake tubing they found in the trailer.

When they finally arrived at the hotel at 1:30 a.m., the guy at the front desk erroneously told Scott and Ken that Kim and I had never checked in. What's more, he told them that there was no record of my even having a reservation for two rooms at the hotel — even though Kim and I checked in with no problem — and made them pay for their own room.

The truck was going to require some additional repair and some cleaning. Numerous harried roadside repairs left the inside of the trailer looking like a tool and grime bomb had exploded in it.

Kim and I began hunting the auto parts stores and dealerships of Oaxaca for the various parts and fluids we needed to bring the truck and the Impala up to snuff. Back at the hotel, Kim dove into the repairs Ken and Scott had outlined for the truck, while I started picking up tools and organizing our stuff inside the trailer. No sooner than I had finished, Scott and Ken were back on the job and ready to start work again. I busied myself tinkering with the Impala, repairing an oil leak and performing a few basic cooling system checks to make sure that everything was working the way it was supposed to.

By 1 p.m., we were ready to make the trek to Puebla, maybe have a nice relaxed evening at some quaint Mexican watering hole and rejoin the race the following morning.

Ha! Yeah, sure.

# Chapter 17
## Is it too late to hire a travel agent?

The highway to Puebla swept us out of the lush tropical jungles and highlands of the south and into the rolling red rocks and scrub brush typical of Central Mexico. We reached the city by dusk and began searching for the hotel and an ATM.

Kim pulled the truck and trailer up to the curb near a bank and we walked back to use the cash machine. I was eager to get some of the native currency as Kim had been footing the bill for tolls, fuel for the truck and food since I ran out of cash, just prior to our arrival in Tuxtla.

The problem was, I had unwittingly dropped my debit card in the hotel parking lot in Oaxaca.

I fumbled through my wallet five or six times in disbelief then walked back to the truck and searched my suitcase for the missing card. Nothing. Now I not only had no money, but some tourist was probably charging souvenir sombreros to my card back in Oaxaca. I wanted to call home and tell Kathy to cancel the card, but I couldn't dial out on my cell phone. More than ever, I was wishing I had visited beautiful Mexico the way normal people do: An all-inclusive resort package, with four buffets a day, bottomless margarita glasses and daytime bus trips to Mayan ruins.

We were too far away to turn back and, just as I had no way to call my wife, I had no way to call the hotel in Oaxaca to ask if anyone had discovered my debit card. So, we pressed on toward the next hotel. By the time we'd reached the heart of the city of Puebla, rain was crashing against the truck and trailer, sounding like nails being poured out of a box onto a tin roof. The hotel was on a downtown street with no parking, so we drove around some more until we found a shopping mall with a big, half-empty parking lot.

By then it was about 8:30 p.m. and we were all ready for the ride to end. We dragged our baggage about a quarter mile to the hotel lobby where I attempted to check us in.

Yup, you guessed it, we were at the wrong hotel. The one we had been assigned was somewhere on the outskirts of the city allegedly near a municipal golf course, we were told. We piled back in the truck and, armed with the directions the clerk had attempted to give us in broken English, as well as a map I had swiped from the lobby, set out to find the correct hotel. After about an hour of wandering through the narrow streets of the city, we flagged down a taxi driver who gladly and quickly led us to the right place.

By the time we arrived, it was after 10 p.m. We had missed the driver's meeting as well as the dinner that the race organizers throw each night. Back in the room, disgusted, discouraged and despondent, I called Kathy, told her about the missing debit card and went to sleep. The sun would come up tomorrow.

Unfortunately, that sun hadn't yet risen over Puebla when we dragged ourselves out of bed and set out to find the race's starting arch.

Much to Kim's chagrin, I agreed with Ken and

Scott to travel in a convoy through the entire day of racing, just to be sure that we didn't get separated again, in the event that the repairs made to the truck didn't hold.

The truck would slow us down to a crawl, but my hope was that we could, at the very least, stay together and possibly even arrive at the next town without Ken having to spend the day sprawled across the truck's engine on his belly like an infantryman ducking enemy fire.

Before we shoved off from the hotel, Scott popped open the truck's hood to make sure its fluids were up to snuff, and found that the motor oil definitely wasn't. A line to the oil cooler had rubbed through and 15W40 had been spraying around the engine compartment lawn-sprinkler-style for who knows how long. Scott cut the line in two and spliced it together with a pipe nipple that happened to be rolling around inside my tool box, then secured it with a pair of hose clamps.

It was still early when we finally hit the road for Morelia, but most of the race cars and crews had already roared off for the starting line which was reportedly in downtown Puebla.

As usual, we were late and lost again.

Knowing full well that we would just wind up wandering around Puebla aimlessly, Kim and I pointed the Impala straight for the highway and the first checkpoint of the day with Ken and Scott on our bumper in the truck. Kim had the foresight to include a set of two-way radios in our survival kit, so he and Ken were in constant communication, navigating.

Even with the truck in tow, we actually managed to stay with the slower cars in the field through Mexico City and arrived at a rest stop at the midway point in Toluca on time.

In the parking lot of a shopping mall in Mexico City, all of the cars still in the race were lined up. Kim and I chose an open parking spot next to a vintage Ferrari easily worth the combined total of all of our worldly assets. After taking full advantage of the free coffee and danishes being served inside one of the sponsors' hospitality tents we saddled up and headed for Morelia, where the day's racing ended.

We left the rest stop early, but wound up arriving in town long after the big inflatable finishing arch had been packed up and the party was over. By bringing up the rear, however, we were able to get a spooky

The Impala draws admiring glances from a couple of guys with excellent taste in cars at the Centro Santa Fe shopping mall in the Mexico City borough, Cuajimalpa. The race stopped there for a brief car show after running as a convoy through Mexico City.

glimpse at the cars that had left the road on the Carrera's treacherous Mil Cumbres speed sections.

Mil Cumbres (Thousand Peaks) pits racers against the devilish twists of a scenic two-lane mountain road that cuts through the pine-covered hills of this popular camping and hiking preserve. It reminded me of northern New York's beautiful Adirondack Park, but at over 9,000 feet the geological giants in Mil Cumbres made the tallest of our Adirondack "high

Jose Rubio, a veteran Carrera competitor who drives an LPG-fueled race car, generously provided us with fuel, free of charge, from the back of his truck throughout the race. Here his crew gives the Impala's engine the once over while topping up the tank. Were it not for Jose, his family and team, we'd still be wondering around Mexico lost and looking for propane.

peaks" (Mount Marcy at 5,344 feet) look like a speed bump. One of the most spectacular wrecks of the event occurred on Mil Cumbres when two Americans lost it on a curve and crashed into a colossal pine tree wadding their car up into a ball. I didn't see workers extracting the car, but Scott said that the big tree prevented them from taking a ride down the face of a sheer bluff. Luckily, both driver and navigator were OK, but undoubtedly shaken up.

# Chapter 18
## Hey Carrera, mind if we tag along?

After dinner, Kim and I climbed back in the Impala and cruised around bustling Morelia in search of an LPG filling station where we could top off the Impala's big, white fuel cylinder.

After a short wait behind a convoy of delivery trucks, the attendant filled the Impala's tank for the equivalent of about $17 U.S. We found that LPG filling stations were pretty common on the outskirts of most of the Mexican towns we passed through, though they aren't state-owned like the Pemex stations throughout the country.

The following day, the race started from the parking

lot of our hotel, so the chances of getting lost looking for the starting line were slim. Kathy had given
the cell phone company hell the previous evening
because I had no phone service in Mexico, though
everyone else did, so now on day four, I could finally
make calls out.

At the previous night's driver's meeting, Ken and
Scott had acquired a genuine service-vehicle route
book, complete with maps and directions. They were
about as confident as they could be that the truck
would make it to the next city, Aguascalientes.

We made it to the starting line on time and roared
off into morning rush hour traffic in our rusted, ill-
handling race car. The morning's race route would
take us back up into the ear-popping heights of Mil
Cumbres for more steering wheel sawing and furious
brake pedal pumping through the twists and turns of
the Thousand Peaks. Unfortunately, we blew straight
past the turn-off for the road to Mil Cumbres on
a two-lane divided highway. So, correcting our mistake meant finding a break in the median to make
a U-turn, driving back toward the turnoff on the
highway's other lanes and then finding another break
in the median for yet another U-turn. We were a good

15 minutes behind by the time we found our way back to the turnoff, so I dropped the hammer to try and catch the tail end of the field.

We wound our way up the snaking mountain road — the temperature was cool, the road wet from a soaking rain the night before and the Impala's delivery-truck engine was in its element. As I had done on previous canyon runs, I hugged the rock face with my front fenders and let the tail of the car find traction — not the most efficient method of driving, but one that I felt safe with. The fact was, the Impala was easy to control in a slide thanks to the weight of the propane cylinder behind the rear wheels and the nose-to-the-clouds attitude of its suspension, both of which seemed to help counter the weight of the massive 348 engine.

We came up fast behind a Federale driving a new Dodge patrol car—not surprising because the Mexican police of all jurisdictions were on hand controlling traffic throughout the race. This was a bad sign though because it meant we were late getting to the first speed stage and all the cars had moved on. This guy was probably blocking traffic at the start of the speed stage and had gotten word to move on to the next stage.

I snuggled the Impala's big chrome front bumper up to his taillights. For a couple of miles, he picked up the pace but then moved over to let us by, giving us a smile and a wave as we roared past, blowing off the posted speed limit.

I kept slipping and sliding the Impala clumsily over the rain slicked mountain road until we caught the pack traveling slowly in a long convoy. I pulled out and passed the last six or eight cars then pulled into line.

Kim had already figured out what was going on: "Mike, we're OK—they must've cancelled the speed sections because of the rain."

Perfect. We weren't totally out of the race despite our driving tour of downtown Morelia earlier that morning. We managed to stay on time and on course until the service stop in Leon, where the race organizers had laid out a lunch spread under a tent outside a restaurant. Ken and Scott were hanging out in the parking lot when we arrived — with no sad tales of mechanical woes to report. As the other racers began pulling out, we decided to head back the way we had pulled into town and fuel up the Impala at a vehicle

LPG station.

For the rest of the day, we straggled along at the rear of the pack. I wasn't exactly driving on the ragged edge, as the terrain had changed radically from the mountainous south to long, desolate stretches of desert highway where it was brutally hot. We were maintaining a stable temperature but dropping further off the pace at every stop. When we arrived at the second-to-last speed stage of the day, everyone had packed up and left. The road ahead was long and straight, flanked by desert plains dotted with scrub brush and baked-out dirt the color of clay fired in a furnace.

I stepped on it and we blew through the desert at over 100 mph. A thunderstorm swept across our path delivering only a trace of rain but some of the most dramatic lightning strikes I had ever seen.

In our haste to find the finish line, we accidentally passed the small asphalt racetrack where the last speed section of the day was being held. We kept racing toward the finish anyway, which was somewhere in the center of the city of Aguascalientes. As we approached a major intersection, we spotted another racer attempting to drive on the right shoulder around some stalled traffic. I aimed for the left shoulder and blew through the red light, passing all of the cars. Then, just up ahead, I saw a local police officer jump in his Nissan patrol car, which had been parked in the median.

Running the Carrera definitely didn't exempt us from traffic laws and I figured we were about to have our first brush with Mexican justice. I also doubted that the cops here would be as benevolent as the Albany police had been when they caught me flouting traffic laws as a teenager. But instead of pulling me over, the cop switched on his lights and sirens and motioned for us to follow him down the two-lane divided main drag.

"He's giving us a police escort!" Kim shouted.

We roared through traffic on the cop's back bumper at 70 to 80 mph. With the police car's lights and sirens blaring, other cars along the way were quickly pulling to the side. As we neared the finish, there were throngs of people on the sides of the road cheering us on. We pulled under the finishing arch for the first time during the race, late but not dead last and a couple of nice kids hung finishing medals around our necks.

It felt to us like we had won the Indy 500 when we pulled into a quaint cobblestone city square where all of the cars were lined up car-show style. There were craft and food vendors all around. Stores and cantinas were open for business and people were everywhere.

This was what the race was supposed to be like! Viva LaCarrera!

The next day, we woke up early in order to check over the car and find some fuel. The start was scheduled for the same place where we finished the previous night, so we weren't concerned about getting lost.

While Ken adjusted the Impala's brakes on a side street alongside the hotel, Scott sent me on a hunt for some gear oil to top off the transmission. I wandered around the city on foot looking for a place to buy some 90-weight oil to no avail and finally bummed some off another racer.

Next, I needed to find fuel. While my inexpensive LPG fuel system had worked flawlessly, fueling up the Impala was a bit of a pain, even in a country where LPG-fueled vehicles were common. Once again, I headed off on foot hoping to find an LPG filling station. I flagged down a police officer on a motorcycle who spoke a little English. He was very patient and

friendly and, once we were clear on what I was asking for, he radioed into his dispatcher for directions
to an LPG station. The officer then began directing
me to the place with gestures and broken English.
Unfortunately, his instructions were too complicated
for a high-school language class failure, unfamiliar
with the city, to understand. So, I just listened, shook
my head as if I knew what he was talking about and
then thanked him profusely, smiling and uttering the
only Spanish word I knew: "Gracias, gracias!"

I started hiking back to the hotel, figuring we were
screwed and would spend the first few hours of the
day riding around aimlessly looking for fuel. But when
I turned a corner on the way back to the hotel, I spotted an LPG tank truck backing into a nearby business,
apparently making a delivery. I ran over to the driver
and tried to explain that I wanted him to fill up my
race car, but it was obvious that he didn't have a clue
what I was asking. I then begged him to wait for me
there and ran down the street to get the Impala.

When I backed the car up to the delivery truck,
the driver smiled and nodded in acknowledgement.
A group of guys came out of the building and gath-
ered around the Impala as he filled it up — they also

seemed pleased with my LPG-fueled racer and made no mention of the crappy body work and paint. That I could understand, anyway.

The driver handed me a ticket from the truck's meter and I gladly paid him the cash. Kim and I suited up and headed back to the bullfighting arena where the race would begin.

Many of the racers had already arrived at the starting line and were milling around outside their machines when we arrived. We pulled up alongside a beautifully prepared Ford Falcon from Sweden that was competing in our class, Historic C, driven by Mats Linden and co-driven by Ralf Christensson.

Linden was a race-winning driver in the Swedish Touring Car Championship series, but his Carrera car had an even more dynamic racing history. The Falcon was a former Holman and Moody prepared rally car that narrowly missed winning the 1963 Monte Carlo rally with Bo Ljungfeldt of Sweden at the wheel.

Linden told me it was a barn find that had been completely restored back to original specs. Though the car probably belonged in a museum, he was out racing it through Mexico the way Holman and Moody intended.

This '63 Falcon Futura was originally built by the legend-
ary race team Holman and Moody and it almost won the
1963 Monte Carlo rally. It was restored and competing in
our class driven by Mats Linden, who was an actual race
car driver. Sure, we stood a chance.

— PHOTO COURTESY OF FORD MOTOR CO.

The Swedes had lost their clutch on the first day of
the Carrera and lost two days getting it repaired. They
had roared passed us dozens of times during the race
and after inspecting the race car, I understood why.
Even 42-year-old Holman and Moody technology was
light years ahead of the race prep job I'd cursed the
Impala with. The Falcon weighed just 2,300 pounds
but was built like a modern day NASCAR stock car

and was powered by a high-strung Ford 289.

Linden managed to keep a straight face when looking over the Impala and actually seemed impressed
when we told him about the LPG fuel system.

"Why did you set the front end up so high?"
he asked sincerely in perfect English with a slight
Swedish accent. "Were you worried about the topes?"

"No, I got a deal on the springs — they were for a
car with air conditioning and I was building this thing
as cheaply as possible," I said.

"Hey, that's good!" Linden said, smiling and nodding approvingly. "And look how far along in the race
you are! You should be proud of yourselves! Many
people with much more invested are out!"

It was true. Sure, we were wandering around lost
and hopelessly confused most of the time, but by
showing up every day, we were second or third from
last instead of dead last like we were at the start. As
long as the car kept starting and we didn't plunge off
a cliff, 75th place was ours for the taking.

# Chapter 19
## Great job! But no, it doesn't count

---

**D**ay five had us making a relatively easy cruise into the picturesque city of Zacatecas. The first speed section of the day was at the Aguascalientes race track we'd missed the day before on the way into town — a tiny bull-ring of a road course with blacktop rough as a cheese shredder and sinister bumps in the turns.

The route book told us to make five laps and then pull into the pits at the marked checkpoint to get our time card signed, which would make the whole section official. Unfortunately, what we read was: "Five laps around a race track! Whoohoo!" We never got to the part about where to get the card signed. Until, that is, we'd blown past the checkpoint.

I really let it all hang out on the track figuring that even I couldn't get us killed on an enclosed course so small it was impossible to get the car into fourth gear.

I roared recklessly around the track displaying some of the sloppiest road racing techniques in the history of the automobile. We were definitely making time, though I had no idea how much of a toll the thrashing was taking on our fragile old race car.

We rolled into the pits, brakes and tires smoldering, and pulled up to a group of officials standing near the infield.

Kim poked the time card out the window at one of the officials standing along pit road, but the guy refused it.

"What? Why not?" I heard Kim say. "You've got to be kidding me! How were we supposed to know that?"

The officials were all looking at each other discussing our situation, shaking their heads and gesturing emphatically.

"What's wrong? What's going on?" I said to Kim.

"They say they don't have our time. That we were

supposed to stop back by the tower."

To the race organizers' credit, the route book explicitly described how you were supposed to exit the race track and where the checkpoint was located. All of which we'd have known, if we'd actually read the route book. Like everything else in life though, it's only clear to me how to do something correctly after I've screwed it up and started over 1,000 or so times.

We pulled back onto the road and headed off to the next checkpoint, but when I stabbed the brakes the first time on the highway, the car pulled violently to the right side. We hopped out to take a look and though we found nothing awry with any of the brake lines or hoses, we noticed that one side of the car had settled a good inch lower than the other. This certainly wasn't a game ender, but it would slow us down even further off the pace. Otherwise, the car seemed to be running great, but a more fatal mechanical problem was just beginning to unravel.

At the next speed section, Team Rubio rejoined the race after relentlessly thrashing to repair the transmission in their Studebaker race car. The breakdown had put him behind even us in the race order, which helped make us feel a little less lonesome. On the final speed section of the day, just outside of Zacatecas, we actually started one position ahead of Jose and Hugo. Struggling with the malfunctioning brakes and constantly in fear of overheating the car, I drove the Impala carefully through a twisting pass known as LaBufa, carved into some desert foothills. Meanwhile, Jose's mighty Studebaker was growing larger and larger in my rearview mirror, hungrily gobbling up the turns that separated us. I slowed down and moved far over to the right so that he wouldn't even have to slow down to pass — Hugo waved as they went roaring by. Just as the Studebaker pulled out of sight, the clouds opened up and a teeming rain poured down, instantly turning the road surface greasy and slick.

The big race tires on Jose's car were useless in the rain and he slowed to a crawl, but I barely had to change my steady-as-she-goes gait. We roared right up on the Studebaker's back bumper and followed Jose and Hugo triumphantly across the finish line. After parking the Impala, we stumbled upon a restaurant and had our first tastes of authentic Mexican cooking.

Scott and Ken had also made it into town unscathed and managed to track us down. We ate and drank for a couple of hours then headed back to the hotel to wash off the road grime.

That evening a huge party of racers and locals assembled in the cobblestone streets and walked en mass to a nearby hotel, built out of an old bullfighting arena, for the driver's meeting. Everyone in the streets was given a small ceramic cup attached to a ribbon that you were supposed to hang around your neck. People circulating through the crowd carrying jugs of Mescale would fill the shot-glass-sized cups whenever they saw you looking dry. We had a great time that night walking along getting pie eyed and swapping adventures with other racers. As things turned out, I'm glad the last night was one of our best.

# Chapter 20
## All's well that ends poorly

***

**T**he following day dawned bright and cool over the beautiful Spanish colonial city. Ken pulled the wheels off the Impala on a side street where we had parked the trailer, and attempted to solve the nasty brake pull that had developed the previous day. It was the sixth day of the Carrera — a so-called rest day with a couple of timed passes back through the winding curves of La Bufa and then a tour of the nearby Corona brewery.

The racers assembled at a Pemex station on the outskirts of town and then rolled single-file back to the closed section of highway. The first speed run took us back toward Zacatecas and we roared through it flawlessly, though the brake pull reared its head as soon as the drums heated up. At a parking lot at the end of the stage, race officials walked from car to car handing out participation certificates with the names of driver and co-driver printed on them.

Kim and I were relaxed for the first time in the entire event and eagerly talked over ideas for our next run at the Carrera: A smaller, lighter car; a better truck and an open trailer; or perhaps we would forgo the truck and trailer altogether and simply build a car so bulletproof that we could leave our support vehicle in Texas and drive the race car to the start of the race, like others had done.

In any event, we would be back and would run a smarter, cheaper and more successful race. Hell, we were capable of a top-five finish in our class — it would just be a matter of remembering the lessons taught by the 5,000 or so dumb mistakes we had made over the previous year and applying them in the appropriate spots.

Good thing I was writing all of this stuff down.

We rolled up to the starting line of the day's second and last speed section. I was going to drive the Impala gingerly so that the brake pull didn't ram us into a guardrail — after all, the next day we would make the 400-mile drive back to Nuevo Laredo and take the final checkered flag of the Carrera. No sense wrecking the Impala now.

On the last straightaway of the speed stage, I felt the car shudder and then, with a loud sickening bang, a tooth broke off the rear axle's pinion gear, punching a hole in the housing. Gear oil streamed out of the axle and covered the exhaust, sending a plume of foul smelling smoke into the air as we crossed the finish line. After a great run, this *American Challenger* had finally plowed into the sand pile.

Though badly hobbled, the mighty Impala limped us to a safe spot well off the highway and out of the flow of traffic. The injury was definitely terminal. It was 1 p.m., we had no replacement parts for the rear axle, and the chances of locating pieces on a Saturday night in Zacatecas were slim to none.

This time, even Kim had to admit there was no going on. He placed a call to Ken on my cell phone and, in an hour, Ken and Scott had cleaned all of our stuff out of our hotel rooms and were on the scene to scoop us up.

The race ended for us and the Impala about 400 miles from the finish when a tooth from the pinion gear blew a hole in the rear axle. Here Kim explains to Ken where to find us so we can load the car back in the trailer and head home.

While we were waiting alongside the road, a friendly American expatriate pulled up behind us to inquire if we needed help. He was originally from Minnesota and had set up a metal fabrication business in Zacatecas specializing in light-truck accessories, like toolboxes and grill guards. He seemed a little home-sick speaking with us about life in the U.S. After only a couple of weeks away from home, even surrounded by friends, I definitely knew how he felt.

With the Impala loaded in the trailer, we headed

north to the border and in 48 hours of straight hammering, stopping only for fuel and a couple of quick meals, we were back in my driveway — exhausted and several thousand dollars poorer, but giddy that we had actually raced in La Carrera Panamericana, despite all of the stupid problems that befell us.

Scott's wife, Lisa, and Billie Jo stopped by to collect their husbands. They definitely seemed happy to see them again after a two-week absence. Kim unhitched the trailer from the truck and drove off — no doubt relieved to finally get the hell away from me. I'm pretty sure he changed his phone number too.

Kathy, The Greatest Wife in the World, welcomed me with a warm hug, kisses and dinner for two.

That night, I slowly backed the ailing Impala off the trailer and into the garage (where it rested for nearly six months.) The following day, I pulled all of my tools, spare parts and assorted gear off the trailer and stacked them in greasy random piles around, inside and on top of the car. With a wince, I pulled the garage door shut behind me.

It hadn't been successful, but it was over and we sure as hell had a lot to talk about. The next time I talked to Kim and Ken, we jabbered incessantly about the Carrera. Scott and his wife put together a collection of Scott's photos and made copies for everyone — some of which they graciously allowed me to reproduce in this book.

About seven months after we had returned, Kim was out at sea working in the engine room of a cargo ship, Ken was deeply involved with a major business expansion at his garage and Scott was back attending to the details of his auto-repair business.

I began rummaging through the many boxes of parts and tools I had carelessly dumped around my garage. The memories came flooding back as I picked through some of the junk. A couple of empty soda and water bottles with Mexican brand names reminded me that I still hadn't learned any Spanish. A collection of tubing and assorted fittings reminded me how Scott and Ken had refused to give up and fixed the pesky clutch line on Kim's truck on the side of the road in Mexico. And the water pump pulley that we had pieced back together and reinforced with a piece of steel in Salem, Virginia, reminded me that no matter how bad things seem early on, don't give up until you've exhausted every possible solution. My father-in-law helped me acquire the pieces I needed to repair the Impala's rear axle (cheap, used cast-off parts, of course) and I reassembled it in my garage one cool early May afternoon. I was eager to drive the Impala again, rust holes, loose steering, marginal brakes, loud exhaust and all. The huge LPG tank in the trunk was still topped off from our last fuel stop — free of charge from the tank of Jose Rubio's delivery truck. I only drove the car four miles from home that day, but I did manage to get it into fourth gear and let the 348 pull — the way it had on some of those impossibly steep Mexican climbs.

The Carrera had gotten the better of all of us. But we weren't beaten. Perhaps someday we would return to Mexico, race the entire grueling event and cross the finish line. Maybe not as champions, but definitely as survivors.

OK, on second thought, maybe not.

# Epilogue

Is there any deeper meaning to be extrapo-
lated from the story of four regular guys from
Upstate New York boldly heading off to compete in a highly dangerous and expensive amateur racing event, with two ill-prepared vehicles, only to fall
400 miles short of the goal?

Can our strange and often confusing experiences
help you lose weight, be a more interesting conversa-
tionalist, a better parent or become financially inde-
pendent?

Um... in a word, no.

However, while preparing for and bumbling

through the world's greatest amateur road race for vintage automobiles, I did learn and relearn a life's worth of lessons that I'm still sorting through, and hope that I never hit my head hard enough to forget any of them.

For instance:

- Don't quit until you have completely exhausted every possible option. No matter how much you feel like snuggling up on the couch with a bag of cheese puffs and a box of wine, just keep plodding onward. Remember, it only takes a couple hundred freak, unlikely occurrences to turn yet another humiliating defeat into a glorious victory. At least that's what people who win a lot keep telling me.

- If you ever want to see who your friends really are, convince them to do something completely stupid, dangerous and expensive, or better yet, all of those things. If they ask for nothing in return and even invite you over to their houses for pie afterward, they're definitely your friends. Make sure you get there on time and don't screw it all up for yourself by saying stupid things.

- Finally, when traveling in Mexico, bring lots of

pesos and keep your eyes open for the signs that say "Autopista." ("Pista! Pista!" as one truck driver tried to tell us.) Those are the main toll roads that might actually get you to your destination on time. Provided of course that your truck or your old, rust-blistered, nose-high, LPG-fueled race car doesn't break down.

# About the Author

Mike McNessor
is an editor at
*Hemmings Motor
News* in Bennington,
Vermont, and lives
in Upstate New York
with his understand-
ing and patient wife

Kathy. He can usually be found messing
around with an old car, truck, motorcycle, etc.
This is his first book.

Printed in Great Britain
by Amazon